CW00369324

Certificate Paper C5

FUNDAMENTALS OF ETHICS, CORPORATE GOVERNANCE AND BUSINESS LAW

For assessments in 2010 and 2011

Practice & Revision Kit

In this December 2009 edition

- Banks of multiple choice questions and separate banks of objective test questions on every syllabus area
- Answers with detailed feedback
- Two mock assessments
- Fully up to date as at 1 December 2009

BPP Learning Media's **i-Pass** product also supports this paper

LEARNING MEDIA

First edition June 2006
Third edition December 2009

ISBN 9780 7517 8077 2
(previous 9780 7517 5184 0)

British Library Cataloguing-in-Publication Data
A catalogue record for this book
is available from the British Library

Published by

BPP Learning Media Ltd
BPP House, Aldine Place
London W12 8AA

www.bpp.com/learningmedia

Printed in the United Kingdom

Your learning materials, published by BPP Learning Media
Ltd, are printed on paper sourced from sustainable, managed
forests.

We are grateful to the Chartered Institute of Management
Accountants for permission to reproduce past examination
questions. The answers to past examination questions have
been prepared by BPP Learning Media Ltd.

Contents

Revising with this Kit

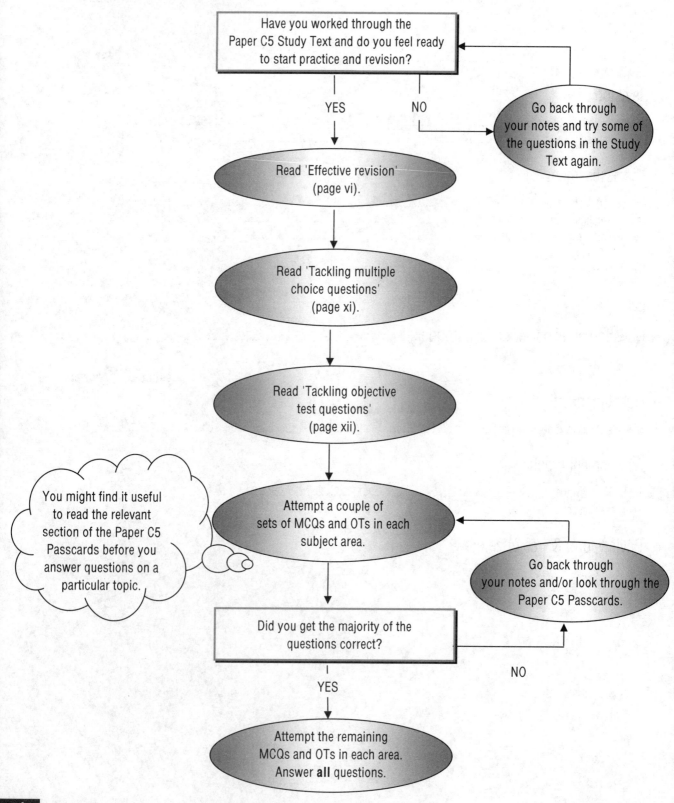

Have you worked through the Paper C5 Study Text and do you feel ready to start practice and revision?

YES

NO

Go back through your notes and try some of the questions in the Study Text again.

Read 'Effective revision' (page vi).

Read 'Tackling multiple choice questions' (page xi).

Read 'Tackling objective test questions' (page xii).

You might find it useful to read the relevant section of the Paper C5 Passcards before you answer questions on a particular topic.

Attempt a couple of sets of MCQs and OTs in each subject area.

Go back through your notes and/or look through the Paper C5 Passcards.

Did you get the majority of the questions correct?

YES

NO

Attempt the remaining MCQs and OTs in each area. Answer **all** questions.

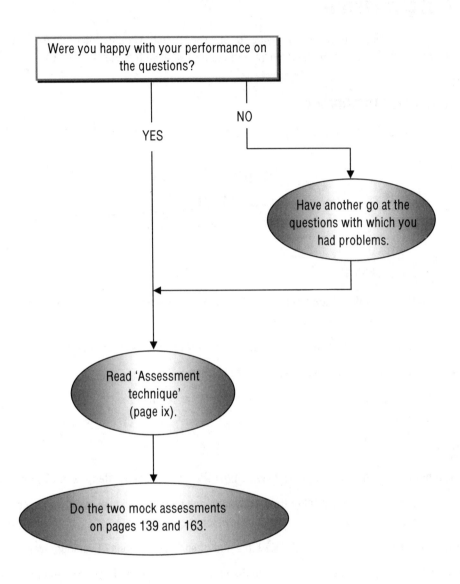

Were you happy with your performance on the questions?

YES

NO

Have another go at the questions with which you had problems.

Read 'Assessment technique' (page ix).

Do the two mock assessments on pages 139 and 163.

Effective revision

This guidance applies if you have been studying for an assessment over a period of time. (Some tuition providers are teaching subjects by means of one intensive course that ends with the assessment.)

What you must remember

Time is very important as you approach the assessment. You must remember:

Believe in yourself

Use time sensibly

Believe in yourself

Are you cultivating the right attitude of mind? There is absolutely no reason why you should not pass this **assessment** if you adopt the correct approach.

- **Be confident** – you've passed exams before, you can pass them again
- **Be calm** – plenty of adrenaline but no panicking
- **Be focused** – commit yourself to passing the assessment

Use time sensibly

1 **How much study time do you have?** Remember that you must **eat**, **sleep**, and of course, **relax**.

2 **How will you split that available time between each subject?** A revision timetable, covering what and how you will revise, will help you organise your revision thoroughly.

3 **What is your learning style?** AM/PM? Little and often/long sessions? Evenings/ weekends?

4 **Do you have quality study time?** Unplug the phone. Let everybody know that you're studying and shouldn't be disturbed.

5 **Are you taking regular breaks?** Most people absorb more if they do not attempt to study for long uninterrupted periods of time. A five minute break every hour (to make coffee, watch the news headlines) can make all the difference.

6 **Are you rewarding yourself for your hard work?** Are you leading a **healthy lifestyle?**

What to revise

You need to spend **most time** on, and practise **lots of questions** on, topics that are likely to yield plenty of questions in your assessment.

You may also find certain areas of the syllabus difficult.

> Difficult areas are
>
> - Areas you find dull or pointless
> - Subjects you highlighted as difficult when you studied them
> - Topics that gave you problems when you answered questions or reviewed the material

DON'T become depressed about these areas; instead do something about them.

- Build up your knowledge by **quick tests** such as the quick quizzes in your BPP Learning Media Study Text and the batches of questions in the i-Pass CD ROM.

- Work carefully through **examples** and **questions** in the Text, and refer back to the Text if you struggle with questions in the Kit.

Breadth of revision

Make sure your revision covers all areas of the syllabus. Your assessment will test your knowledge of the whole syllabus.

How to revise

There are four main ways that you can revise a topic area.

Write it!
Read it!
Teach it!
Do it!

Write it!

Writing important points down will help you recall them, particularly if your notes are presented in a way that makes it easy for you to remember them.

Read it!

You should read your notes or BPP Learning Media Passcards actively, testing yourself by doing quick quizzes or Kit questions while you are reading.

Teach it!

Assessments require you to show your understanding. Teaching what you are learning to another person helps you practise explaining topics that you might be asked to define in your assessment. Teaching someone who will challenge your understanding, someone for example who will be taking the same assessment as you, can be helpful to both of you.

Do it!

Remember that you are revising in order to be able to answer questions in the assessment. Practising questions will help you practise **technique** and **discipline**, which can be crucial in passing or failing assessments.

1   Start your question practice by doing a couple of sets of objective test questions in a subject area. Note down the questions where you went wrong, try to identify why you made mistakes and go back to your Study Text for guidance or practice.

2   The **more questions** you do, the more likely you are to pass the assessment. However if you do run short of time:

   • Make sure that you have done at least some questions from every section of the syllabus

   • Look through the banks of questions and do questions on areas that you have found difficult or on which you have made mistakes

3   When you think you can successfully answer questions on the whole syllabus, attempt the **two mock assessments** at the end of the Kit. You will get the most benefit by sitting them under strict assessment conditions, so that you gain experience of the vital assessment processes.

   • Managing your time
   • Producing answers

BPP Learning Media's *Learning to Learn Accountancy* gives further valuable advice on how to approach revision. BPP Learning Media has also produced other vital revision aids.

• **Passcards** – Provide you with clear topic summaries and assessment tips

• **i-Pass CDs** – Offer you tests of knowledge to be completed against the clock

• **MCQ cards** – Offer you practise in MCQs

You can purchase these products by visiting www.bpp.com/cima

Assessment technique

Format of the assessment

The assessment will contain 75 questions to be completed in 2 hours. The questions will be a combination of multiple choice questions and other types of objective test questions.

Passing assessments

Passing assessments is half about having the knowledge, and half about doing yourself full justice in the assessment. You must have the right approach to two things.

> **The day of the assessment**
>
> **Your time in the assessment room**

The day of the assessment

1   Set at least one **alarm** (or get an alarm call) for a morning assessment.

2   Have **something to eat** but beware of eating too much; you may feel sleepy if your system is digesting a large meal.

3   Allow plenty of **time to get to the assessment room**; have your route worked out in advance and listen to news bulletins to check for potential travel problems.

4   **Don't forget** pens and watch. Also make sure you remember **entrance documentation** and **evidence of identity**.

5   Put **new batteries** into your calculator and take a spare set (or a spare calculator).

6   **Avoid discussion** about the assessment with other candidates outside the assessment room.

Your time in the assessment room

1   **Listen carefully to the invigilator's instructions**

Make sure you understand the formalities you have to complete.

2   **Ensure you follow the instructions on the computer screen**

In particular ensure that you select the correct assessment (not every student does!), and that you understand how to work through the assessment and submit your answers.

3   Keep your eye on the time

In the assessment you will have to complete 75 questions in 120 minutes. That will mean that you have roughly 1.6 minutes on average to answer each question. You will be able to answer some questions instantly, but others will require thinking about. If after a minute or so you have no idea how to tackle the question, leave it and come back to it later.

4   Label your workings clearly with the question number

This will help you when you check your answers, or if you come back to a question that you are unsure about.

5   Deal with problem questions

There are two ways of dealing with questions where you are unsure of the answer.

(a)   **Don't submit an answer.** The computer will tell you before you move to the next question that you have not submitted an answer, and the question will be marked as not done on the list of questions. The risk with this approach is that you run out of time before you do submit an answer.

(b)   **Submit an answer**. You can always come back and change the answer before you finish the assessment or the time runs out. You should though make a note of answers that you are unsure about, to ensure that you do revisit them later in the assessment.

6   Make sure you submit an answer for every question

When there are ten minutes left to go, concentrate on submitting answers for all the questions that you have not answered up to that point. You won't get penalised for wrong answers so take a guess if you're unsure.

7   Check your answers

If you finish the assessment with time to spare, check your answers before you sign out of the assessment. In particular revisit questions that you are unsure about, and check that your answers are in the right format and contain the correct number of words as appropriate.

> BPP Learning Media's *Learning to Learn Accountancy* gives further valuable advice on how to approach the day of the assessment.

Tackling multiple choice questions

The MCQs in your assessment contain a number of possible answers. You have to **choose the option(s) that best answers the question**. The three incorrect options are called distracters. There is a skill in answering MCQs quickly and correctly. By practising MCQs you can develop this skill, giving you a better chance of passing the assessment.

You may wish to follow the approach outlined below, or you may prefer to adapt it.

Step 1   **Note down how long** you should allocate to each MCQ. For this paper you will be answering 75 questions in 120 minutes, so you will be spending on average about 1.6 minutes on each question. Remember however that you will not be expected to spend an equal amount of time on each MCQ; some can be answered instantly but others will take time to work out.

Step 2   **Attempt each question**. Read the question thoroughly.

You may find that you recognise a question when you sit the assessment. Be aware that the detail and/or requirement may be different. If the question seems familiar read the requirement and options carefully – do not assume that it is identical.

Step 3   Read the four options and see if one matches your own answer. Be careful with numerical questions, as the distracters are designed to match answers that incorporate **common errors**. Check that your calculation is correct. Have you followed the requirement exactly? Have you included every stage of a calculation?

Step 4   You may find that none of the options matches your answer.

- **Re-read the question** to ensure that you understand it and are answering the requirement
- **Eliminate any obviously wrong answers**
- **Consider which of the remaining answers** is the **most likely** to be correct and select the option

Step 5   If you are still unsure, **continue to the next question**. Likewise if you are nowhere near working out which option is correct after a couple of minutes, leave the question and come back to it later. Make a note of any questions for which you have submitted answers, but you need to return to later. The computer will list any questions for which you have not submitted answers.

Step 6   **Revisit questions** you are uncertain about. When you come back to a question after a break you often find you are able to answer it correctly straight away. If you are still unsure have a guess. You are not penalised for incorrect answers, so **never leave a question unanswered!**

Tackling objective test questions

What is an objective test question?

An objective test (**OT**) question is made up of some form of **stimulus**, usually a question, and a **requirement** to do something.

- **MCQs.** Read through the information on page (xi) about MCQs and how to tackle them.

- **True or false**. You will be asked if a statement is true or false.

- **Data entry**. This type of OT requires you to provide figures such as the correct figure for payables in a statement of financial position, or words to fill in a blank.

- **Multiple response.** These questions provide you with a number of options and you have to identify those that fulfil certain criteria.

OT questions in your assessment

CIMA is currently developing different types of OTs for inclusion in computer-based assessments. The timetable for introduction of new types of OTs is uncertain, and it is also not certain how many questions in your assessment will be MCQs, and how many will be other types of OT. Practising all the different types of OTs that this Kit provides will prepare you well for whatever questions come up in your assessment.

Dealing with OT questions

Again you may wish to follow the approach we suggest, or you may be prepared to adapt it.

Step 1   Work out **how long** you should allocate to each OT. Remember that you will not be expected to spend an equal amount of time on each one; some can be answered instantly but others will take time to work out.

Step 2   **Attempt each question**. Read the question thoroughly, and note in particular what the question says about the **format** of your answer and whether there are any **restrictions** placed on it (for example the number of words you can use).

       You may find that you recognise a question when you sit the assessment. Be aware that the detail and/or requirement may be different. If the question seems familiar read the requirement and options carefully – do not assume that it is identical.

Step 3   Read any options you are given and select which ones are appropriate. Check that your calculations are correct. Have you followed the requirement exactly? Have you included every stage of the calculation?

Step 4   You may find that you are unsure of the answer.

- Re-read the question to ensure that you understand it and are answering the requirement
- Eliminate any obviously wrong options if you are given a number of options from which to choose

Step 5   If you are still unsure, **continue to the next question**. Make a note of any questions for which you have submitted answers, but you need to return to later. The computer will list any questions for which you have not submitted answers.

Step 6   Revisit questions you are uncertain about. When you come back to a question after a break you often find you are able to answer it correctly straight away. If you are still unsure have a guess. You are not penalised for incorrect answers, so **never leave a question unanswered!**

Useful websites

The websites below provide additional sources of information of relevance to your studies for *Fundamentals of Ethics, Corporate Governance and Business Law.*

- BPP   www.bpp.com

   For details of other BPP material for your CIMA studies

- CIMA   www.cimaglobal.com

   The official CIMA website

- The Times   www.timesonline.co.uk

- Financial Times   www.ft.com

- The Economist   www.economist.com

- Law Society   www.lawsociety.org.uk

- UK Government   www.direct.gov.uk

- The Incorporated Council of Law Reporting   www.lawreports.co.uk

Question and Answer checklist/index

The headings in this checklist/index indicate the main topics of questions, but questions often cover several different topics.

		Page number	
		Question	Answer
Multiple choice and objective test questions			
1	English and alternative legal systems 1	3	99
2	English and alternative legal systems 2	5	100
3	English and alternative legal systems 3	7	100
4	English and alternative legal systems 4	9	101
5	English and alternative legal systems 5	11	102
6	Establishing contractual obligations 1	12	102
7	Establishing contractual obligations 2	14	103
8	Establishing contractual obligations 3	16	104
9	Establishing contractual obligations 4	19	105
10	Performing the contract 1	21	105
11	Performing the contract 2	23	106
12	Performing the contract 3	26	107
13	Performing the contract 4	29	108
14	Contractual breakdown 1	31	108
15	Contractual breakdown 2	33	109
16	Contractual breakdown 3	36	110
17	Contractual breakdown 4	38	111
18	Employment 1	41	111
19	Employment 2	43	112
20	Employment 3	45	113
21	Employment 4	46	113
22	Company formation 1	49	114
23	Company formation 2	51	115
24	Company formation 3	53	116
25	Company formation 4	55	117
26	Company formation 5	57	118
27	Company formation 6	59	119
28	Company administration and management 1	61	120
29	Company administration and management 2	63	121
30	Company administration and management 3	65	122
31	Company administration and management 4	67	123
32	Company administration and management 5	69	123

BPP
LEARNING MEDIA

Questions

1 English and alternative legal systems 1

1   In a criminal case, what is the normal burden of proof placed upon the prosecution?

     A   Beyond any doubt
     B   Beyond reasonable doubt
     C   Beyond every reasonable doubt
     D   Balance of probabilities

2   Which **three** of the following statements about sources of law are **correct**?

     ☐   The principle that once a court has made a ruling on a particular case, then the same decision will be reached in any future similar case, forms the basis of delegated legislation.

     ☐   The term 'case law' is used to describe judge-made laws stemming from courts' decisions.

     ☐   European Regulations become law in member nations without the member nation having to pass legislation.

     ☐   In the United Kingdom, legislation is introduced into Parliament by the Crown.

     ☐   Equity is a source of the law of trusts

3   Which **three** of the following statements about the structure of the English court system are **correct**?

     ☐   All criminal cases, regardless of their gravity, are introduced in the Magistrates' court.
     ☐   The County Court hears civil and criminal cases.
     ☐   The Court of Appeal binds all courts below it and also normally itself.
     ☐   The House of Lords (Supreme Court for the United Kingdom) only hears civil cases if the point of law is in the public interest.
     ☐   The Queens Bench Division of the High Court deals with company law cases.

4   Which of the following European law pronouncements does not have the force of legislation?

     A   Regulation
     B   Recommendation
     C   Decision
     D   Directive

5   Which of the following statements does **not** describe an aspect of tort?

     A   Certain acts constitute an infringement of a person's rights and their commission leads to a claim for compensation by the wronged party.

     B   A person has a number of separate legal rights and an action may be brought at law to assert that a particular right has been infringed.

     C   Certain acts are prohibited by law and their commission leads to prosecution by the state.

     D   A person has a duty at civil law not to infringe the rights of other persons.

6   The Court of Appeal is bound by the previous decisions in the UK of:

   A   The House of Lords (Supreme Court for the United Kingdom) only.

   B   The House of Lords (Supreme Court for the United Kingdom) and a Divisional Court of the High Court only.

   C   The House of Lords (Supreme Court for the United Kingdom) and the Court of Appeal only.

   D   The House of Lords (Supreme Court for the United Kingdom), the Court of Appeal and a Divisional Court of the High Court only.

7   Which of the following describes the 'golden rule' of statutory interpretation?

   A   A statute should be construed to avoid manifest absurdity or contradiction.
   B   Words in a statute should be given their ordinary meaning.
   C   A statute should be interpreted in such a way to give the intended legal effect.
   D   Words in a statute should be interpreted in their intended context.

8   Before a High Court judge is required to apply a previous decision to the case actually before him, he must:

   (i)   Decide whether the decision is binding or merely persuasive.

   (ii)   Distinguish the *obiter dicta* from the *ratio decidendi* and apply the former in his reasoning.

   (iii) Determine that the material facts of the two cases are similar.

   (iv)   Be convinced that the decision was made by a court of higher status than the County Court or Magistrates' Court.

   A   (i) and (iii) only
   B   (ii) and (iv) only
   C   (i), (ii) and (iii) only
   D   (i), (iii) and (iv) only

9   Concern has been raised by a government minister regarding the issue of some statutory instruments. How should the courts seek to control this delegated legislation?

   A   Strike out the legislation if it is contrary to public policy.
   B   Declare the legislation ultra vires and therefore void.
   C   Require a review by a government joint select committee.
   D   Issue an injunction under equitable principles.

10   Which of the following procedures of the European Parliament is used to agree proposals with the Council of Ministers?

   A   Consultation
   B   Review
   C   Co-decision
   D   Assent

2 English and alternative legal systems 2

1   In which of the following would a claim by an employee for discrimination by an employer be heard?

    A   The Court of Appeal
    B   A court of first instance
    C   A Crown Court
    D   An Employment Tribunal

2   The criminal law aims to:

    A   Compensate injured parties
    B   Recover property which has been taken from the true owner
    C   Enforce legal obligations
    D   Penalise wrongdoers

3   All the following statements relate to sources of law. Which one of the statements is **correct**?

    A   Under the principle of judicial precedent, a judge must follow all previous decisions.
    B   The European Parliament is the main source of legislation in the United Kingdom.
    C   The European Court of Human Rights has no authority in the UK.
    D   A bye-law made by a local authority is an example of delegated legislation.

4   Which of the following best describes the meaning of *ratio decidendi*?

    A   A statement of the law applicable to the facts of the particular case which forms the basis of the judge's decision.
    B   The verbatim text of the judgement in a full law report.
    C   A rule of evidence whereby a court will assume the existence of a certain state of affairs without the need for proof.
    D   The approval by or on behalf of the Crown to a bill which has been passed in both Houses of Parliament.

5   All the following statements about sources of law are untrue except one. Which one of the statements is **correct**?

    A   Common law is the name used for all laws stemming from the decisions of the House of Commons.
    B   Some local authorities possess the delegated power to enact bye-laws.
    C   Judicial precedent requires that once any court has made a ruling, the same decision must be reached in all other similar court cases where the material facts are the same.
    D   Decisions of the European Commission are legally binding on all persons and business within the European Union.

6   In respect of audited accounts, to whom does an auditor owe a duty of care not to act negligently?

    A   The shareholders only

    B   The company only

    C   Anyone who relies on the accounts for investment purposes

    D   The company and the shareholders only

---

7   Fill in the missing words.

The .... is formed of commissioners from member states, one of its roles is to fulfil the European Union's executive function.

The .... contains members directly elected from member states and it supervises the other EU institutions.

The .... is formed of Heads of State from member states.

The .... applies EU law and provides decisions and rulings that are binding on the parties involved in the case.

European Council	European Court of Justice
European Parliament	European Commission

---

8   Which **three** of the following elements must be present for a duty of care to exist?

    ☐   There must be a sufficient relationship of proximity between defendant and claimant.

    ☐   It must be reasonable that the defendant should foresee that damage might arise from his carelessness.

    ☐   The claimant must have acted in good faith.

    ☐   It must be just and reasonable for the law to impose liability.

    ☐   The claimant must have acted without carelessness.

---

9   Nicholas works as a foreman in a cement processing factory. Vats of chemicals are used to clean the raw materials entering the process. The materials are kept in asbestos containers in a separate part of the plant. During processing the lid of one of these containers falls into a vat near to Nicholas. He is splashed by the chemical and, before he can get away, the vat explodes following a reaction between the asbestos and the chemical previously unknown to science. Nicholas, barely alive after the explosion, brings a claim in tort against the employers. Will he succeed?

	Splash	*Explosion*
A	No – too remote	No – too remote
B	Yes – foreseeable	Yes – foreseeable
C	Yes – foreseeable	No – too remote
D	No – too remote	Yes – foreseeable

---

10   When an auditor audits a limited company, what standard of care does he owe?

    A   That of the common man

    B   That of a reasonable and competent auditor

    C   That which can be reasonably expected from him, personally, as an auditor

    D   Foreseeable care

3 English and alternative legal systems 3

1   Which of the following European institutions sets EU strategy and policy?

    A   The European Parliament
    B   The European Commission
    C   The European Council
    D   The European Court of Justice

2   Melanie and Jane go out to lunch together at Rumsey's Restaurant. Melanie is buying lunch for Jane as a treat, so Melanie orders and also pays the bill. The same night Jane has to be admitted to hospital as she is suffering severe food poisoning as a result of eating a negligently prepared mussel at the restaurant. Jane wishes to claim damages for the distress suffered and the fact that she had to take three weeks away from her self-employment.

What is the legal position?

    A   Jane cannot sue Rumsey's Restaurant as she does not have a contract with it.

    B   Jane can sue Melanie, as it is Melanie who ordered and paid for the bad mussel. Melanie must then sue the restaurant.

    C   Jane can sue Rumsey's Restaurant as she was owed a duty of care by the restaurant, which has breached that duty.

    D   Jane cannot sue either the restaurant or Melanie, as by eating the mussel she consented to the risk of food poisoning.

3   Fill in the missing words.

Most legislation in the UK is in the form of .... Acts. These differ from .... Acts which concern powers granted to individuals and institutions.

.... Acts confer power to delegated bodies and are also known as delegated legislation. ....
legislation places case law onto a statutory basis.

Codifying	Public
Private	Enabling

4   Which of the following are types of delegated legislation?

    (i)   Orders in Council
    (ii)   Regulations of the European Union
    (iii)   Statutory instruments
    (iv)   Acts of Parliament
    (v)   Local authority bye-laws

    A   (i), (ii) and (iii) only
    B   (i), (iii) and (v) only
    C   (ii), (iii) and (v) only
    D   (ii), (iii), (iv) and (v) only

5   In negligence for misstatements which result in economic loss to the claimant, what forms the basis of the existence of a legal duty of care?

A   Foreseeability only
B   Proximity only
C   Foreseeability and proximity
D   Foreseeability and damage

6   Statements made *obiter dicta* are:

A   Binding in lower courts as they are principles of law relating to the facts of the case.
B   Binding in courts 'at the same level' hearing similar cases.
C   Not binding unless they are made by the European Court of Justice.
D   Not binding at all.

7   Which **three** of the following statements correctly complete this sentence?

In order to show that there exists a duty of care not to cause financial loss by negligent misstatement, the claimant must show that:

☐   The person making the statement did so in an expert capacity of which the claimant was aware.

☐   The context in which the statement was made was such as to make it likely that the claimant would rely on it.

☐   In making the statement the defendant foresaw that it would be relied upon by the claimant.

☐   The claimant considered the statement.

☐   The claimant was not insured for financial loss.

8   Which of the following are criminal proceedings?

A   A divorce action
B   An action by a claimant for £1 million damages for fraudulent misrepresentation
C   An action by a claimant for breach of contract
D   A prosecution prompted by the CPS for non-payment of tax

9   Delegated legislation is drawn up under powers conferred by the full Parliament in Acts. Which of the following statements concerning delegated legislation are **correct**?

(i)   The power to make such legislation may be delegated to local authorities.

(ii)   Ministerial powers are exercised by Orders in Council, a common form of delegated legislation.

(iii) Parliament may not revoke an enabling act.

(iv)   Legislation laid before Parliament for 40 days without a negative resolution being passed in respect of it automatically comes into force.

A   (i) and (iv) only
B   (ii) and (iii) only
C   (i), (ii) and (iv) only
D   (i), (iii) and (iv) only

10   Which of the following presumptions are 'canons of statutory interpretation'?

(i)   An Act of Parliament applies only to England and Wales unless otherwise stated.
(ii)   An Act of Parliament does not have retrospective effect.
(iii)   For a criminal offence to be committed, there must be intention on the part of the accused.
(iv)   An Act of Parliament does not bind the Crown.

A   (i) and (iii) only
B   (ii) and (iv) only
C   (i), (ii) and (iv) only
D   (ii), (iii) and (iv) only

4 English and alternative legal systems 4

1   Sri Lanka operates a penal code based on which country's law?

A   China
B   England
C   India
D   France

2   Executive orders and agency rules are forms of delegated legislation in which country?

A   England
B   USA
C   Germany
D   China

3   Criminal law is a common type of:

A   Private law
B   Procedural law
C   Public law
D   International law

4   The court structure of which of the following countries consists of a trial level, an appeal level and a supreme level?

A   Germany
B   France
C   Denmark
D   Italy

5   Fill in the missing words.

Some legal cases are taken up by the government and are against private individuals (or vice versa), such actions are known as .... law actions.

Disputes concerning contracts, tort or company law that are between parties in the same legal system are known as .... law actions.

Cases between parties who are from different legal systems come under .... law.

Access to the legal system, the rights of disputing parties and rules on the submission of evidence are examples of .... law.

Procedural	Private
Public	International

6   What is the name of the Polish lower house of Parliament?

A   Sejm
B   Senate
C   Sabah
D   Congress

7   International customary law is based on principles known as:

A   Common principles
B   Common custom
C   Binding norms
D   Accepted practice

8   Which statement(s) concerning the role of judges is/are **correct**?

A   Judges under Sharia law cannot create law.
B   Judges under codified systems cannot create law.
C   Judges under codified systems can be involved in judicial review.
D   All of the above.

9   In the USA, what is the consequence when state law conflicts with federal law?

A   State law will prevail.
B   Federal law will prevail.
C   The matter is referred to the Federal courts to decide which shall prevail.
D   State law prevails but the matter can be appealed to the United States Supreme Court.

10   Under Sharia law, which **three** of the following are forbidden?

☐   Consumption of pork
☐   Apostasy
☐   Blasphemy
☐   Mashtur
☐   Madhab

5 English and alternative legal systems 5

1   Which of the following are the key principles in a civil law system?

    A   Certainty and codification
    B   Certainty and commonality
    C   Comprehensibility and certainty
    D   Comprehensibility and codification

2   Which of the following are key sources of international law?

    A   Treaties and regulations
    B   Treaties and conventions
    C   Directives and treaties
    D   Constitutions and customs

3   Which type of law is **not** codified in France?

    A   Administrative law
    B   Criminal law
    C   Tort
    D   Contract

4   In the Italian legal system, what is the name of the legislative chamber consisting of members who have been elected nationally?

    A   Congress
    B   The Senate
    C   Parliament
    D   House of Representatives

5   Which of the following are sources of Danish law?

Select all that apply.

- [ ] Constitutional Acts
- [ ] Acts of Parliament
- [ ] Sharia law
- [ ] Case law
- [ ] Custom law

6   In codified (civil) law systems, judges have which of the following roles?

    A   To draft new statutes
    B   To apply the letter of the law
    C   To bring the government to account where the law does not meet the needs of the people
    D   To interpret international law

7   The Chinese legal system can be traced back to which important historical figure?

    A   Plato
    B   Confucius
    C   Hannibal
    D   Alexander the Great

8   In the Russian legal system, disputes between businesses are heard by:

    A   The regular courts
    B   Courts of Arbitration
    C   The Constitutional Court
    D   District courts

9   Which of the following statements is **correct**?

    A   Sharia law contains moral and legal obligations.
    B   Statutes under common law are simple documents of general principles.
    C   Statutes under codified systems are complex documents.
    D   Judges under codified systems are bound by decisions in previous cases.

10   The Five Pillars of Islam categorise a Muslim's actions. Which of the following is **not** a legitimate category?

    A   Meritorious
    B   Reprehensible
    C   Forbidden
    D   Acceptable

6 Establishing contractual obligations 1

1   A Ltd has been induced to enter a contract with B Ltd by the latter's negligent misrepresentation.

Which of the following is **incorrect**?

    A   A Ltd may sue B Ltd for damages in the tort of negligence.
    B   A Ltd may sue B Ltd for damages under the Misrepresentation Act 1967.
    C   A Ltd may sue B Ltd for damages in the tort of deceit.
    D   A Ltd may treat the contract with B Ltd as voidable.

2   Consider the following chain of events. Is there a contract?

1 April	Amy sends a letter to Beth offering to sell her a bicycle for £100.
3 April	Amy changes her mind and writes to Beth informing her that the offer is no longer open.
4 April	Beth receives Amy's offer letter and writes back to accept.
5 April	Beth receives Amy's second letter.
7 April	Amy receives Beth's letter of acceptance which she returns, unread.

A   No. Amy has revoked the offer by the time that Beth accepts it by writing to Beth. Beth cannot accept a revoked offer.

B   Yes. Beth can accept the offer until she receives notice of the revocation.

C   No. Amy has not read the acceptance, therefore she has not agreed to it.

D   No. Beth has given no consideration.

---

3   One party has been induced to enter into a contract by a negligent misrepresentation of the other party. Which of the following is **incorrect**?

A   If rescission is available, damages in lieu may be awarded at the court's discretion under the Misrepresentation Act 1967.

B   Rescission cannot be ordered if it is impossible to return the parties to their pre-contract position.

C   Despite being the victim of a misrepresentation, the misrepresentatee may affirm the contract.

D   For this type of misrepresentation, damages may be obtained under the tort of negligence but not under the Misrepresentation Act 1967.

---

4   Which of the following examples of performance amounts to good consideration?

(i)   The performance of an existing duty under general law
(ii)   The performance of an existing contract in return for a promise by a third party
(iii)   The performance of an act, followed by a promise to pay for that act

A   (i) only
B   (ii) only
C   (i) and (ii) only
D   (iii) only

---

5   An act which has already been performed before an act or promise is given in return is not usually sufficient as consideration. But it will be where:

A   A person performs a service at another's request and is later promised payment.
B   A person spends money on his own initiative and another party later agrees in writing to repay it.
C   A debt has become statute-barred but the debtor verbally acknowledges its existence.
D   A promissory note is given in settlement of an existing debt.

---

6   Tim offered to sell a stereo system to Neil for £200 on 2 September saying that the offer would stay open for a week. Neil told his brother that he would like to accept Tim's offer and, unknown to Neil, his brother told Tim of this on 3 September. On 4 September Tim, with his lodger present, sold the stereo to Ingrid. The lodger informed Neil of this fact on the same day. On 5 September Neil delivered a letter of acceptance to Tim. Is Tim in breach of contract?

A   No. Neil delayed beyond a reasonable time and so the offer had lapsed by the time Tim sold to Ingrid.

B   No. Neil was told by a reliable informant of Tim's effective revocation before Neil accepted the offer.

C   Yes. Tim agreed to keep the offer open and failed to do so.

D   Yes. Tim was reliably informed of Neil's acceptance on 3 September so his sale to Ingrid on 4 September is breach of contract.

---

7 Which of the following statements is **correct**?

(i) The parties to a social or domestic arrangement are presumed to have intended the arrangement to be legally enforceable.

(ii) The parties to a commercial transaction are presumed not to have intended the arrangement to be legally enforceable.

A (i) only
B (ii) only
C Both (i) and (ii)
D Neither (i) nor (ii)

8 Maud goes into a shop and sees a price label for £20 on an ironing board. She takes the board to the checkout but the till operator tells her that the label is misprinted and should read £30. Maud maintains that she only has to pay £20. How would you describe the price on the price label in terms of contract law?

A An offer
B A tender
C An invitation to treat
D An acceptance

9 Consideration:

(i) Must be of adequate and sufficient value
(ii) Must move from the promisee
(iii) May be the performance of an existing contractual duty
(iv) Must be provided at the time the contract is made

A (i) only
B (ii) only
C (ii), (iii) and (iv) only
D (iii) and (iv) only

10 Alexander wrote to Brian and offered to sell him his set of antique cigarette cards for £300. Brian wrote back that he accepted the offer and would pay for them in two instalments of £150. Is there a contract?

A Yes. There is offer, acceptance and consideration. The contract is valid.
B No. Alexander's letter was not an offer but an invitation to treat.
C No. Until Alexander receives Brian's letter, the acceptance is not valid.
D No. Brian's letter has varied the terms and so is a counter-offer, rejecting Alexander's original offer.

7 Establishing contractual obligations 2

1 Which of the following is an offer?

A An advertisement in the newsagent's window
B An invitation to tender
C An auction bid
D An exhibition of goods for sale

2   A fraudulent misrepresentation renders a contract:

    A   Valid
    B   Void
    C   Voidable
    D   Illegal

3   If a creditor makes a promise, unsupported by consideration, to a debtor that the creditor will not insist on full discharge of a debt and the promise is made with the intention that the debtor should act on it and he does so, the creditor cannot retract his promise unless the debtor can be restored to his original position. This illustrates which of the following?

    A   Revocation
    B   Promissory estoppel
    C   Misrepresentation
    D   Past consideration

4   Miranda owes Emma £500 for her wedding dress. Emma, because she is in need of cash, agrees to accept £400 in full settlement of the debt, but she later claims the full amount. Will she succeed?

    A   No. Miranda's payment is full consideration for Emma's promise to waive her rights.

    B   No. She is estopped from retracting her promise.

    C   Yes. Because Miranda took advantage of Emma's financial problems.

    D   Yes. She had no intention that Miranda should act on the waiver and so the doctrine of promissory estoppel does not apply.

5   Which of the following is **not** an essential element of a valid simple contract?

    A   The contract must be in writing.
    B   The parties must be in agreement.
    C   Each party must provide consideration.
    D   Each party must intend legal relations.

6   A Ltd has been induced to enter into a contract with B Ltd by the fraudulent misrepresentation of C Ltd, a third party.

Which of the following is **correct**?

    A   A Ltd may sue C Ltd for damages in the tort of deceit.
    B   A Ltd may sue C Ltd for damages under the Misrepresentation Act 1967.
    C   A Ltd may recover damages from C Ltd for breach of contract.
    D   A Ltd may treat the contract with B Ltd as void.

7   Francis buys a table from Matthew for £100, who believes it to be worthless. Francis knows that it is very valuable. Neither party discloses his belief to the other. Later Matthew discovers that Francis has sold the table for £750,000, to another party in good faith. What is his remedy?

   A   Rescind the contract and sue for damages under the Misrepresentation Act 1967 for negligent misrepresentation.

   B   Rescind the contract and sue for damages for innocent misrepresentation.

   C   Sue for damages under the tort of deceit.

   D   Matthew has no remedy.

8   Which of the following statements is **incorrect**?

   A   If an agreement is of a commercial nature, it is presumed that the parties intend legal relations.

   B   If an agreement is of a commercial nature, the parties cannot argue that there was no intention to create legal relations.

   C   Even if an agreement is of a commercial nature, it is open to the parties to show that legal relations were not intended.

   D   Even if a commercial agreement is in writing, it is open to the parties to show that legal relations were not intended.

9   A Ltd wrote to B Ltd offering to sell the company specified items of plant and machinery and requiring acceptance of the offer by fax. Which of the following is **correct**?

   A   The acceptance is complete as soon as the fax is sent by B Ltd.
   B   The acceptance is complete as soon as A Ltd receives the fax.
   C   The contract cannot be concluded by fax.
   D   Acceptance by fax is subject to the 'post rules'.

10   In relation to misrepresentation, which of the following statements is **incorrect**?

   A   As a general rule silence cannot amount to misrepresentation.
   B   The misrepresentee cannot claim damages if he has affirmed the contract.
   C   A person cannot rely on the misrepresentation if it did not induce him to contract.
   D   A half-truth may amount to a misrepresentation.

8 Establishing contractual obligations 3

1   Which of the following are essential requirements of a contract?

   (i)   Offer and acceptance
   (ii)   Consideration
   (iii) Written contractual terms
   (iv)   Intention to create legal relations

   A   (i), (ii), (iii) and (iv)
   B   (i), (ii) and (iii)
   C   (i), (ii) and (iv)
   D   (i), (iii) and (iv)

2   Which of the following cannot be carried out by a simple contract?

    A   A contract for the sale of a motor car

    B   A contract of employment

    C   A contract for the sale of land

    D   A contract for the provision of services

3   Samantha offered to sell her car to Patrick for £2,000. She said he could think about it until Monday. Patrick rang her on Saturday and left a message on her machine asking if she would agree to his paying in monthly instalments for six months. She rang back in the evening to say she would want the full cash sum. On Sunday, Patrick accepted the original offer. Meanwhile, Samantha had sold the car to Iain on Saturday night.

What is the legal position?

    A   Patrick's telephone message amounted to a counter-offer which was a final rejection of the original offer.

    B   Patrick's telephone message was a counter-offer but he still had an option on the car until Monday.

    C   Patrick's telephone message was merely a request for information, but as he and Samantha did not yet have agreement, she was free to sell the car to someone else.

    D   Patrick's telephone message was a request for information only, Samantha had not revoked the offer, so his acceptance on the original terms means they have a contract.

4   Bill's will states that his son, Ben, should have use of his house during Ben's life. The executors allowed Ben to occupy the house in accordance with Bill's wishes and for nominal rent of £1 per quarter.

The executors later decide it would be better to sell the house. They claim that Ben has no right to stay in the house because he has not provided any consideration against their promise that he can stay.

Which of the following statements summarises the **correct** legal position?

    A   The executors are right. The nominal rent is a past act and there is no consideration to allow Bill to stay now.

    B   The executors are right. Bill has provided consideration in paying the nominal rent, but it is not the market rent and therefore he will have to leave.

    C   The executors are wrong. Bill has provided sufficient consideration in paying the nominal rent and he will be allowed to stay on the strength of their promise.

    D   The executors are wrong due to the wishes of the deceased which are expressed in the will.

5   Elizabeth decides to sell her string of pearls to Mary and writes to her on 24 February, offering her the string of pearls for £250. At the same time, Mary decides that she wants the pearls and writes to her on 24 February, offering to buy them for £250.

Before either of these letters are received, Mary sees a similar necklace in a shop for £200 and decides to buy that instead.

What is Mary's legal position?

    A   She is contracted to buy Elizabeth's necklace as they have agreement.

    B   She is not contracted to buy Elizabeth's necklace as there is no consideration.

    C   She is not contracted to buy Elizabeth's necklace as her offer does not constitute acceptance of Elizabeth's offer of sale.

    D   She will only be able to avoid contracting with Elizabeth if she speaks to her before Elizabeth receives her letter.

6   Laine is selling her house to Catherine. They are about to exchange contracts. All the searches have been completed, but then Laine finds out that a shopping centre is going to be built on the land to the side of the house. She has previously told Catherine that she did not know of any such development plans.

May Catherine claim for misrepresentation if the contracts are exchanged now?

A   No, because silence cannot be construed as misrepresentation.
B   Yes, because what Laine has told Catherine has become misleading.
C   No, because Catherine should have found that out on her own behalf.
D   Yes, because with contract for property, all known facts must be stated.

7   In the absence of express statements as to whether or not legal relations are intended:

A   The courts always assume that legal relations were not intended.
B   The courts assume that legal relations were not intended unless they were social arrangements.
C   The courts will assume that legal relations were intended unless the parties can prove otherwise.
D   The courts assume that legal relations were intended in commercial cases unless proved otherwise.

8   David made an offer by fax which he sent from Singapore. Katy received this fax in London, just prior to getting on a plane to New York. Katy was keen that the contract should be sealed so she faxed an acceptance to David from New York. As he had flown from Singapore to Sydney, she faxed him there.

Where was the contract made?

A   Singapore. David made the offer there.
B   London. Katy received the offer there.
C   New York. Katy faxed her acceptance there.
D   Sydney. David received the acceptance there.

9   Simon is keen to buy some second hand golf clubs. His friend, Dave, advises him to talk to Lee, who is trying to sell a set. Lee tells Simon that he will sell his set for £250. Simon is unsure, because the golf clubs are better and more expensive than he intended buying. He asks Lee if he can tell him in a couple of days. Lee agrees.

Two days later, Simon rings Dave to discuss whether or not to buy the golf clubs. Dave tells him that Lee has changed his mind about selling them. Simon rings Lee up straight away and agrees to buy the clubs for £250.

Is there a contract?

A   Yes, because Lee has promised to keep the offer open.
B   No, because Simon's request to keep the offer open for a couple of days was too vague to be binding.
C   No, because Dave has told Simon of Lee's intentions and the offer has been revoked.
D   Yes, because Lee needed to tell Simon himself that he wasn't going to sell the clubs any more.

10 The law of contract is of special importance in providing a legal framework within which businesses can operate.

Which one of the following statements is **correct**?

A   A contract need not necessarily be in writing.
B   The consideration provided by the two parties to a contract must be of equal value.
C   A contract comes under the remit of criminal law rather than civil law.
D   A contract can be entered into validly by all persons.

9 Establishing contractual obligations 4

1   Which of the following statements about the law of contract is **correct**?

A   Providing an agreement is in writing, it will always form a valid contract.
B   Cases involving breach of contract are normally heard in the Crown Court.
C   An agreement between two parties to undertake a criminal act is not a legally-recognised contract.
D   An agreement between two businesses to allow late payment for goods or services is not an example of a contract.

2   Deb was induced to enter into a contract by the negligent misrepresentation of Dave. The contract was to buy three concert tickets.

Deb wants rescission of the contract. Which of the following is **incorrect**?

A   Deb must tell Dave that she wishes to rescind the contract.
B   If Deb has sold one of the tickets to an innocent third party she cannot rescind the contract.
C   Deb will only be granted rescission within a reasonable time from the date of the contract.
D   Deb is not entitled to rescission because Dave's misrepresentation was not fraudulent.

3   An agreement to carry out an act which the law requires anyway amounts to:

A   Sufficient consideration
B   Insufficient consideration
C   Past consideration
D   Proper consideration

4   What is executory consideration?

A   An act or forbearance
B   A promise of an act or forbearance
C   Consideration performed on the basis of a promise made
D   Consideration provided by an act performed before the contract is made

5   Which of the following contracts must be made by deed?

A   An assignment of a debt
B   A sale of shares
C   A consumer credit contract
D   A 25 year lease

6   Karl is interested in buying Marcus's car. Marcus is in trouble with his creditors and so is keen to sell. In the course of correspondence, Marcus refuses Karl's offer of £3,000 but states that 'for a quick sale, I will accept £4,000. Please let me know immediately if you are not interested at this price.' Karl accepted this price verbally which Marcus acknowledged.

Later, Marcus, having come into some money, denies that he has made an offer, but that he was providing information about acceptable prices to Karl.

What is the legal position?

A   Marcus was only providing information to Karl about prices and this does not constitute an offer for the purposes of contract.

B   In the context, it was clear that Marcus was making an offer of sale for that price which Karl has accepted, so they have a valid contract.

C   In the context, it was clear that Marcus was making an offer of sale for that price, however, Karl's acceptance was only verbal and therefore not valid, so they have not got a contract.

D   Marcus has made an offer and Karl has accepted, so they have a contract, but Marcus can avoid the contract because Karl has not yet provided the consideration of £4,000.

7   Which of the following statements is **correct**?

(i)   In an agreement of a social or domestic nature it is presumed that the parties intend to create legal relations.

(ii)   In a commercial agreement it is presumed that the parties do not intend to create legal relations.

(iii)   In a commercial agreement it is presumed that the parties do intend to create legal relations.

(iv)   In an agreement of a social or domestic nature it is presumed that the parties do not intend to create legal relations.

A   (i) and (ii)
B   (i) and (iii)
C   (ii) and (iv)
D   (iii) and (iv)

8   Misrepresentation results in a contract being:

A   Void
B   Voidable
C   Invalid
D   Valid

9   Which of the contracts below is a standard form contract?

A   An oral agreement between two parties who have negotiated terms regarding the standards of performance to be met by each party in the main contract.

B   An oral agreement to enter into relations on the basis of conditions and warranties as agreed following negotiations between the parties.

C   A document signed by both parties to a contract in which contractual conditions and warranties as negotiated between them are set down.

D   A document put forward for the customer's signature by a supplier of goods in which pre-printed contractual conditions and warranties are set out.

10   Jude goes into a shop and sees a price label for £200 on a dishwasher. She agrees to buy the dishwasher but the till operator tells her that the label is misprinted and should read £300. Jude maintains that she only has to pay £200. How would you describe the price on the price label in terms of contract law?

A   An acceptance
B   An invitation to treat
C   An offer
D   A tender

10 Performing the contract 1

1   Dee Ltd has broken one of the terms of its contract with E Ltd. If that term is a condition, which of the following is **correct**?

A   E Ltd is entitled to damages only.
B   E Ltd is entitled to sue for damages or to repudiate the contract.
C   E Ltd is only entitled to repudiate the contract.
D   E Ltd may repudiate the contract and sue for damages.

2   The Sale of Goods Act 1979 implies a number of terms into consumer contracts. Which of the following are terms it implies?

A   Title, quantity, fitness
B   Title, sale by sample, price
C   Description, price, fitness
D   Description, quality, fitness

3   Which of the following statements is **incorrect** in relation to the Unfair Contract Terms Act 1977?

A   A consumer is not someone who makes the contract in the course of a business.
B   One party does make the contract in the course of a business.
C   The goods which are the subject of the contract are any type to be used for any purpose excluding business purposes.
D   The goods which are the subject of the contract are of a type ordinarily supplied for private use or consumption.

4   If a seller has title in respect of the goods they are selling then:

A   They have complete legal ownership of the goods.
B   They have the right to act as distributor of the goods only.
C   They can prevent a buyer from selling the goods after they have purchased them.
D   They are responsible for replacing or repairing the goods if they are faulty.

5   Which of the following statements concerning contractual terms are **incorrect**?

(i)   Terms are usually classified as either conditions or warranties, but some terms may be unclassifiable in this way.

(ii)   If a condition in a contract is not fulfilled the whole contract is said to be discharged by breach.

(iii)   If a warranty in a contract is not fulfilled the whole contract is said to be discharged by breach, but either party may elect to continue with his performance.

(iv)   Terms which are implied into a contract by law are never contractual conditions.

A   (i) and (ii) only
B   (iii) and (iv) only
C   (i), (ii) and (iii) only
D   All of them

6   The Unfair Terms in Consumer Contracts Regulations 1999 provide that any terms which create a 'significant imbalance' in the rights and obligations of the parties to a standard form contract are not binding on a consumer. 'Consumer' means:

A   Any natural person acting for the purposes of a trade, business or profession.
B   Any natural person acting outside the purposes of any trade, business or profession.
C   Any natural person or company acting for the purposes of a trade, business or profession.
D   Any natural person or company acting outside the purposes of any trade, business or profession.

7   Grace and Geoffrey are both opera singers. They have each contracted with Opera Organisers Ltd to attend rehearsals for a week and then appear in the two month long run of a new production. Due to illness, Grace did not attend the rehearsals or the opening night but recovered sufficiently to appear by the fourth night. Due to illness, Geoffrey was unable to attend for the first four days of rehearsals. Opera Organisers Ltd have booked substitutes for both Grace and Geoffrey for the entire run.

What is the legal position?

A   Both Grace and Geoffrey are in breach of a condition of their contract and both of their contracts with Opera Organisers are completely discharged.

B   Grace is in breach of condition of her contract, but Geoffrey is in breach of warranty only and his contract is not discharged.

C   Grace is in breach of warranty and her contract is not discharged, while Geoffrey is in breach of condition, so his contract is discharged.

D   Neither Grace nor Geoffrey are in breach of condition. They are both in breach of warranty, so neither contract is discharged.

8   Dee Ltd has broken one of the terms of its contract with E Ltd. If that term is a warranty, which of the following is **correct**?

A   E Ltd may repudiate the contract with Dee Ltd.
B   E Ltd can avoid the contract and recover damages.
C   E Ltd is entitled to sue for damages only.
D   E Ltd is entitled to sue for damages or to repudiate the contract.

9   Adam wants to buy a house from Steve. Steve's neighbour is Simon. Steve has regularly had to ask Simon to moderate the noise coming from his house and has recently even involved the police on the grounds of noise pollution. While Adam was looking around the house, he asked Steve what the neighbours were like. Steve replied that he didn't see much of them.

Adam buys the house and discovers when he moves in that Simon is a difficult and noisy neighbour. Adam proposes to sue Steve for misrepresentation.

What is the legal position?

A   Steve is not liable for misrepresentation as he gave a statement of opinion, not fact.

B   Steve is liable for misrepresentation as he had a duty to give an answer to Adam's question which was complete enough not to give a misleading impression.

C   Steve is liable for misrepresentation as the contract was one of extreme good faith.

D   Steve had no duty to disclose what he knew, Adam should have been a more careful buyer.

10   In which of the following situations has an actionable misrepresentation **not** occurred?

A   Peter, who wants to sell an antique vase, tells Paul, incorrectly, that it is Wedgwood, knowing that Paul will pass the information on to John, whose wife collects Wedgwood. John buys the vase.

B   Thomas makes a gun, hiding a defect with a metal plug. Matthew buys the gun without inspecting it. It later explodes and injures Matthew.

C   Judas is selling his arable farm to Andrew. He states, when questioned, that it would support 2,000 sheep, although he has never used it for sheep farming. This proves to be untrue.

D   Noah is selling his vet's practice to Shep. At the start of negotiations, he stated that it was worth about £30,000 a year. He then fell ill and custom fell away. When Shep took over, it was worth about £5,000.

11 Performing the contract 2

1   Wincey purchases a nylon and polyester electric blanket from Sleeptight Ltd by mail order. The contract contains the following clauses purporting to exclude Sleeptight's liability.

(i)   'We accept no liability for death or personal injury caused by this product except where our negligence is proved.'

(ii)   'The limit of our liability for loss or damage caused by this product is that of the enclosed Customer Guarantee.'

(iii) 'We accept no liability for breach of Section 14 of Sale of Goods Act 1979.'

(iv)   'The product supplied under this contract satisfies the description applied to it by the catalogue and no liability attaches to the company if this is not so.'

(v)   'Any defect in the company's title to sell the product is not to affect the validity of this contract.'

Which of these exclusion clauses will be void if Wincey is (1) a consumer and (2) a business customer?

	(1) Consumer	(2) Business customer
A	(i), (iii) and (v) only	(i) and (v) only
B	(iii), (iv) and (v) only	(v) only
C	(ii), (iii), (iv) and (v) only	(v) only
D	All of them	(i) and (v) only

2   Which of the following statements is **correct**?

    (i)   Any contract may be made in any form.
    (ii)   Oral contracts must always be evidenced in writing.
    (iii)   A deed for land transfer must always be in writing and signed.
    (iv)   A transfer of shares must be in writing.

    A   (i) and (ii)
    B   (ii) and (iv)
    C   (iii) and (iv)
    D   (i) and (iv)

3   Sian is negotiating with a manufacturer to buy stock for her new shop 'Kind Bath'. She will be selling a range of toiletries and bathroom items. She has explicitly told her shampoo manufacturer during the course of discussions that she does not want to buy goods tested on animals or that have had ingredients tested on animals. The manufactured replied that the products were not tested on animals.

    Sian sold some of the goods in her shop, advertising them as kind to animal products. An animal rights group pointed out that one of the ingredients in the shampoo range had been tested on animals. Sian took the rest of the product off her shelves and refused to pay the supplier.

    What is Sian's legal position with regard to her contract with the supplier?

    A   The fact that Sian did not want her stock to be tested on animals was discussed before the contract but not expressly incorporated into the contract. The contract is valid.

    B   The supplier has misrepresented the issue of the animal testing, but Sian may not rescind the contract as she has sold some of the goods.

    C   Sian's representation that she would not buy products tested on animals was intended to be a term of the contract. The supplier has breached the contract.

    D   The contract has been breached under the implied terms as to description under the Sale of Goods Act 1979.

4   By virtue of the Unfair Contract Terms Act 1977, an attempt by any person to exclude or restrict his liability for damage to property caused by negligence is:

    A   Void unless reasonable

    B   Effective only in a non-consumer transaction

    C   Void

    D   Valid if the other party to the contract knows of the exclusion clause or has been given reasonable notice of it

5 Which of the following statements concerning contractual terms are **correct**?

 (i) Terms are usually classified as either conditions or warranties, but some terms may be unclassifiable in this way.

 (ii) If a condition in a contract is not fulfilled the whole contract is said to be discharged by breach.

 (iii) If a warranty in a contract is not fulfilled the whole contract is said to be discharged by breach, but either party may elect to continue with his performance.

 (iv) Terms which are implied into a contract by law are always contractual conditions.

 A (i) and (ii) only
 B (iii) and (iv) only
 C (i), (ii) and (iv) only
 D All of them

6 Which of the following methods is **not** an effective way to determine the price in a contract in which the details are incomplete?

 A A clause stating it to be 'on usual hire purchase terms'
 B Price to be set at that ruling in the market on the day of delivery
 C An arbitrator to set the price
 D Price to be set by course of dealing between the parties

7 Michael cannot read. He buys a railway ticket on which is printed 'conditions – see back'. The back of the ticket stated that the ticket was subject to conditions printed in the timetables. These included an exclusion of liability for injury. During Michael's journey, a suitcase fell off the racks and injured him.

 What is the legal position?

 A The ticket office contained no notice of the conditions of carriage and the railway could not rely on the notice given on the back of the ticket.

 B The conditions are contained in the timetable. As such, they are adequately communicated and the railway can avoid liability.

 C The railway cannot rely on Michael being able to read. The conditions should have been communicated to him verbally and the railway cannot avoid liability.

 D The railway cannot rely on the notice disclaiming liability as the contract had been made previously and the disclaimer was made too late.

8 What is an exclusion clause?

 A It is a contractual warranty that the terms of the contract will be performed.

 B It is a clause excluding the rights of persons other than the contracting parties to sue for breach of contract.

 C It is a clause which limits the contractual capacity of one of the parties.

 D It is a contractual clause which limits or excludes entirely a person's obligation to perform a contract or his liability for breach of contract.

9   During negotiations before entering into a contract for the sale of a car Howard says to Hilda 'the car will be ready for collection on the day you require it'. This statement is described as:

    A   A representation

    B   A term

    C   A warranty

    D   An advertiser's puff

10   Which of the following factors is **not** identified by the Sale of Goods Act 1979 to be an aspect of the quality of goods?

    A   Fitness for all purposes

    B   Freedom from minor defects

    C   Durability (ie satisfactory quality for a reasonable period)

    D   Finish and appearance

12 Performing the contract 3

1   The Unfair Contract Terms Act 1977 provides that an attempt by any person to exclude or restrict his liability for death or personal injury resulting from negligence in any contract is:

    A   Void unless reasonable

    B   Effective only in a non-consumer transaction

    C   Void

    D   Valid if the other party to the contract knows of the exclusion clause or has been given reasonable notice of it

2   Harriet bought an expensive coat from 'Coats are us'. She has exceptionally sensitive skin and the coat gave her a painful rash. Harriet is claiming that the coat was not fit for the purpose under the Sale of Goods Act 1979. What is the legal position?

    A   There is only one obvious purpose for a coat and it has failed in that purpose. Harriet is correct.

    B   Harriet has relied on the skill and judgement of the shop assistants, who have provided her with a product that doesn't meet her needs. Harriet is right.

    C   The Sale of Goods Act does not apply to this transaction. Harriet is wrong.

    D   There was a peculiarity connected with this purchase which Harriet should have brought to the attention of the shop assistants. Harriet is wrong.

3   Which of the following statements is **incorrect** in relation to the implied terms of the Sale of Goods Act concerning description?

    A   If a description is applied to the goods, it is a sale by description.

    B   There is an implied condition that the goods correspond to the description.

    C   All descriptive words used form part of the contract terms.

    D   Description is interpreted to include ingredients, age, date of shipment, packing and quantity.

4   Lenny is the managing director of Hoodwink Ltd, a computer games developer. One day he purchases a company car from Cut and Shut Motors Ltd. Under the terms of the contract, Cut and Shut Ltd excluded any liability for mechanical problems. The next day, the car's exhaust systems falls off. What is the legal position of Hoodwink Ltd?

A   The contract is of a commercial nature and therefore the clause stands and Hoodwink has no right of redress.

B   Hoodwink is classed as a consumer, therefore the clause is not allowed under the Unfair Terms in Consumer Contracts Regulations.

C   Hoodwink must mitigate the cost of repairs.

D   The Sale of Goods Act does not apply to motor vehicles therefore Hoodwink must pay for the repairs itself.

5   Anne was induced to enter into a contract to purchase goods by the negligent misrepresentation of Bob. Anne seeks rescission of the contract.

Which of the following is **incorrect**?

A   Rescission is a court order requiring a contract to be correctly carried out.
B   Anne will be granted rescission only if she applies within a reasonable time.
C   The remedy may be refused if Anne has acted inequitably herself.
D   Anne will lose the right to rescind if an innocent third party acquires rights to the goods.

6   Which of the following is **incorrect** under the fitness for purpose provisions of the Sale of Goods Act 1979?

A   A buyer must make known the particular purpose for which he wants the goods, unless the goods have only one obvious purpose.

B   Where there is a peculiarity about the intended purpose for goods, the buyer must make the seller aware of that peculiarity.

C   The buyer must be explicit in his description of the purpose for which he wants the goods.

D   To claim that the goods supplied are not fit for the intended purpose, it must be shown that the buyer relied on the seller's skill and judgement, even if only partially.

7   What is the effect of the '*contra proferentem*' rule?

A   A person who signs a written contract is deemed to have notice of and accepted the terms contained in it in the absence of misinformation as to their meaning.

B   A person who seeks to enforce an exclusion clause in a consumer contract must show that it is reasonable.

C   The working of an exclusion clause will generally, in the absence of absolute clarity, be construed against the party seeking to rely on it.

D   The court acts on the presumption that an exclusion clause was not intended to work against the main purpose of the contract.

8   A term may be implied into a contract:

(i)   By statute

(ii)   By trade practice unless an express term overrides it

(iii)   By the court to provide for events not contemplated by the parties

(iv)   By the court to give effect to a term which the parties had agreed upon but failed to express because it was obvious

(v)   By the court to override an express term which is contrary to normal custom

A   (ii) and (iii) only
B   (i), (ii) and (iv) only
C   (i), (iv) and (v) only
D   (i), (iii), (iv) and (v) only

9   Katie took her wedding dress to the dry cleaners to be cleaned. It was a silk dress, made with intricate beading and sequins. She was given a receipt which contained conditions, which she was told restricted the cleaner's liability, particularly with regard to the risk of damage to the beads and sequins on her dress. The conditions actually stated that the cleaners had absolutely no liability for damage to the dress. Katie signed the agreement assuming that all dry cleaners would want to protect themselves against damaging beads and sequins.

The dress was badly stained in the cleaning process.

What is Katie's legal position?

A   She signed the document restricting the cleaner's liability so she is bound by its terms.

B   The conditions have been adequately communicated and so are binding regardless of her signature.

C   She was misled by the cleaners as to the extent of the exclusion clause and so she is not bound by the terms.

D   She is not bound by the terms because they were not made available to her at the time of the contract.

10   If one party announces his intention not to honour his agreement before the performance was due, this is called:

A   Misrepresentation
B   Fundamental breach
C   Substantial performance
D   Anticipatory breach

13 Performing the contract 4

1   The effect of signing a document is:

(i)   The person signing is prima facie assumed to have read the document.
(ii)   The person signing the document is bound by all its terms, irrespective of what they provide.

Which is/are **correct**?

A   (i) only
B   (ii) only
C   Both (i) and (ii)
D   Neither (i) nor (ii)

2   Henry agreed to sell his horse to Richard at a given price. When the negotiations were over and the contract formed, Henry told Richard that the horse was sound and 'free from vice'. The horse turned out to be vicious and Richard wants to bring an action against Henry.

Richard will fail in his action because Henry's promise that the horse was not vicious was:

A   A statement of opinion not fact
B   Made after the original contract and was not supported by consideration
C   Not relied upon by Richard
D   Merely a 'sales puff'

3   John owes Catherine £26.89. Kathleen, John's mum, agrees to pay Catherine £20 on John's behalf and Catherine accepts it 'in full settlement'. Two weeks later, Catherine requested the remaining £6.89 from John. Is she entitled to the money?

A   Yes, because part payment does not provide sufficient consideration for a promise to discharge a debt.
B   Yes, because a third party cannot absolve others of their liability under a contract.
C   No, because part payment by a third party is good consideration for a promise to discharge a debt.
D   No, because intervention by a relative was not intended to be a legal act.

4   A Ltd has broken one of the terms of its contract with B Ltd. If that term is a warranty, which of the following is **correct**?

A   B Ltd may repudiate the contract and claim damages.
B   B Ltd may repudiate the contract and apply for rescission.
C   B Ltd is entitled to damages only.
D   B Ltd is entitled to damages and rescission.

5   Which of the following statements is **correct**?

A   A breach of condition entitles an innocent party to repudiate a contract unless he has accepted the breach.

B   A breach of a condition entitles an innocent party to repudiate a contract whether or not the breach has been accepted.

C   A breach of a condition entitles an innocent party to recover damages only.

D   A breach of a condition or warranty entitles the innocent party to damages only.

6   In a contract for the sale of goods between a business and a consumer, any attempt to exclude the terms implied by the Sale of Goods Act 1979 is:

A   Void

B   Void unless reasonable

C   Voidable at the option of the consumer

D   Valid if the consumer is given written notice of the clause

7   Grace owes Rebecca £40, which must be paid by 1 January. Rebecca really needs some money to do some Christmas shopping so she tells Grace that if she pays her at the beginning of December, she only has to pay £25, 'in full satisfaction of the debt'. Rebecca doesn't get as much Christmas money as she was hoping for and starts to wish, on 26 December, that she had asked Grace for the full amount.

Can Rebecca claim the remaining £15 from Grace?

A   Yes. However, she will have to wait until 1 January as that is when Grace will be breaching the contract.

B   Yes. She can claim it from Grace and Grace must pay her by 1 January.

C   No. Rebecca is bound in honour not to claim her legal rights.

D   No. Grace provided consideration for part payment by paying early, therefore Rebecca has no rights under the old contract.

8   Which of the following statements relating to contract terms is **incorrect**?

A   Contract terms are usually classified as either conditions or warranties, but some terms may be unclassifiable in this way.

B   A breach of warranty gives the injured party the right to rescission and to claim damages.

C   A breach of condition gives the injured party the right to terminate the contract and claim damages.

D   Some contract terms may be implied by custom, statute or the courts.

9   Jack and Jill visited Bognor Regis and booked into a hotel for the night. On arriving in their room they noticed that there were many conditions of contract pinned to the back of the door, including clauses limiting liability by the hotel for loss of valuables which were not placed in the hotel safe. Jack and Jill had never seen these conditions before. Which of the following is **correct**?

A   The hotel has adequately disclosed the exclusion clause and Jack and Jill are bound by the conditions.

B   Jack and Jill have signed for their room at reception, so the conditions are binding on them.

C   The hotel has given them a misleading explanation of the terms, so Jack and Jill are not bound by the terms, even though they have signed for them.

D   Jack and Jill are not bound by the terms, because the contract was made before they reached the room, so the hotel cannot rely on the exclusion clause.

10   Which of the following is **incorrect**?

A   An exclusion clause must be incorporated into a contract before the contract has finally been concluded.

B   An exclusion clause may be invalidated by the Unfair Contract Terms Act 1977, in a case to which the Act applies.

C   If a person signs a document containing an exclusion clause he is held to have agreed to it, even if he has not read the document, unless he has been misled about the term's legal effect.

D   Under the *contra proferentem* rule, when deciding what an exclusion clause means, the courts interpret any ambiguity in the favour of the person who relies on the exclusion.

14 Contractual breakdown 1

1   Which of the following statements regarding anticipatory breach is **incorrect**?

A   Anticipatory breach automatically discharges the contract.
B   A person's genuine mistake will not necessarily repudiate a contract.
C   Action for breach can be delayed until actual breach occurs.
D   Subsequent events can affect the injured party's right to action.

2   The general rule for a contract to be discharged by performance is that performance must be exact and precise. Which of the following is **not** an exception to that rule?

A   Where time is not of the essence
B   Where the promisee prevents performance
C   Where the contract is substantially performed
D   Where the contract is partially performed

3   Where there has been anticipatory breach of contract the injured party is entitled to sue:

A   After a reasonable time.

B   Only from the moment the other party actually breaches a contractual condition.

C   From the moment the other party indicates that he does not intend to be bound.

D   From the moment the injured party has fulfilled his obligations but the other party indicates that he does not intend to be bound.

4   In an action for breach of contract, the court will **not** award:

A   Damages for financial loss
B   Unliquidated damages
C   Liquidated damages
D   Damages identified in a penalty clause

5   Which of the following is a genuine cause of a contract being frustrated?

A   Personal disinclination to perform a contract of personal service.
B   Non-occurrence of an event which is part of the purpose of the contract.
C   Personal incapacity to perform a contract of personal service.
D   Increase in the cost of meeting contractual terms.

6   Rosie and Jim were married and owned their marital home jointly. Jim left the home, to go and live with his secretary. The spouses met to discuss their situation and Jim agreed to pay Rosie £750 a month. She agreed to pay the mortgage payments and Jim agreed to transfer the house to Rosie's sole possession when the mortgage was paid off. Rosie requested Jim to put the agreement into writing and to sign it, which he did.

Rosie paid off the mortgage and Jim refused to transfer the house into her name.

What is the position?

A   Rosie has not provided consideration for the agreement as all the money used to pay off the mortgage has come from Jim both before and after he left the marital home.

B   Rosie and Jim are married so the courts will assume that there was no intention to create legal relations.

C   Rosie and Jim are separated so the courts will presume that legal relations were intended and Jim will have to transfer the property.

D   The courts will assume legal relations but the consideration is inadequate due to all the mortgage payments that Jim made prior to leaving the marital home.

7   Which of the following statements is **correct**?

A   Damages are an equitable remedy and are primarily intended to restore the party who has suffered loss to the same position he would have been in if the contract had been performed.

B   Damages are a common law remedy and are primarily intended to restore the party who has suffered loss to the same position as he would have been in if the contract had been performed.

C   Damages are an equitable remedy whereby the court orders a person to perform a contract so that the other party to the contract does not suffer loss.

D   Damages are a common law remedy whereby the court orders a person to perform a contract so that the other party to the contract does not suffer loss.

8   Daniel owns a mill. The main crank shaft of the mill has broken and it has to be sent to London to be used by specialist manufacturers as a pattern for a new one. Daniel contracts with Lionel to transport the broken shaft to London.

Lionel neglects to take the shaft to London on his next delivery, and the shaft does not get repaired and returned to Daniel for two weeks, when it was supposed to have taken one week. During that time, the mill has been out of operation as it cannot run without its main crank shaft. Daniel claims loss of profits against Lionel.

Which of the following is **correct**?

A   The claim must fail. Daniel's loss could not reasonably be foreseen by Lionel.

B   The claim will succeed for the second week. Lionel was contracted to deliver within a certain time and might reasonably have known that delay would inconvenience Daniel.

C   The claim must fail. Damages are not awarded for loss of profits, but only for expenses arising from the breach. Daniel has incurred no extra expenses.

D   The claim will succeed in part. Only nominal damages will be awarded as the claim is speculative and it is impossible to ascertain the loss.

9   Cee Ltd ordered goods from Dee Ltd to be delivered to F Ltd.

If the goods are not delivered,

A   F Ltd can sue Dee Ltd for breach of contract.

B   Cee Ltd can sue Dee Ltd for breach of contract and recover compensation for its own loss.

C   Cee Ltd may sue Dee Ltd for breach of contract and recover compensation for its own loss and the loss to F Ltd.

D   Cee Ltd can sue Dee Ltd for breach of contract only if it was acting as the agent of F Ltd.

10   Which of the following statements is/are **correct**?

(i)   The limitation period for claims for breach of contract may be extended if a debt or other certain monetary amount is acknowledged or paid in part before the original period of limitation has expired.

(ii) The claim must be acknowledged as existing by the defendant. This does not have to be in writing.

A   (i)
B   (ii)
C   Both (i) and (ii)
D   Neither (i) nor (ii)

15 Contractual breakdown 2

1   Which of the following statements concerning limitation to actions for breach is **incorrect**?

A   The right to sue for breach of contract is usually statute barred after six years from the date on which the cause of action accrued.

B   The right to sue for breach of contract by deed is statute barred after twelve years from the date on which the cause of action accrued.

C   If the defendant is of unsound mind at the time of the contract, the six year period begins to run when his disability ceases or he dies.

D   If the information relevant to possible claims is deliberately concealed, the normal period of six years can be extended after the period of six years has started to run.

2   Which of the following is **not** an equitable right in contractual breakdown?

A   Rescission
B   Specific performance
C   *Quantum Meruit*
D   Injunction

3   Which of the following statements is/are **correct**?

   (i)   The purpose of an injunction is to enforce a negative restraint in a contract.

   (ii)   The purpose of an injunction is to restrain acts which appear inconsistent with the contract's obligations.

   A   (i)
   B   (ii)
   C   Both (i) and (ii)
   D   Neither (i) nor (ii)

---

4   Chill 'n' Freeze is a supplier of hotel mini-bars. One of its customers, Posh Hotels, is seeking damages due to faulty bars which leaked chemicals into hotel rooms.

   Under the commercial contract, Chill 'n' Freeze excluded liability for indirect and consequential losses.

   Posh Hotels want damages for the loss of profit they would have made if the mini-bars worked correctly.

   What is Chill 'n' Freeze's legal position?

   A   No liability for loss of profit as the damage is consequential.
   B   The term is unfair under the unfair contract terms act, so Chill 'n' Freeze is liable for the loss of profit.
   C   Partial liability as Posh Hotels did not mitigate its loss.
   D   Liable for the loss of profit as it is directly attributable to the breach.

---

5   Which of the following statements is **incorrect**?

   A   The courts will award damages for mental distress if that is the main result of the breach.

   B   The general principle of damages is to compensate for actual financial loss.

   C   The amount of damages awarded is only that which puts the claimant in the position he would have been in but for the breach.

   D   Damages may only be awarded for losses arising naturally from the breach which arise in a manner the parties may reasonably be supposed to have contemplated.

---

6   Which of the following is **not** a definition of the doctrine of frustration of contract?

   A   Parties should be discharged from their contract if altered circumstances render the contract fundamentally different in nature from what was originally agreed.

   B   Parties should be discharged if an event, for which neither party is responsible and which was not contemplated occurs, which renders the contract fundamentally different and which results in a situation to which the parties did not originally wish to be bound.

   C   Parties who contract that something should be done are discharged if performance becomes impossible.

   D   Parties who contract that something should be done are discharged if their assumption that certain conditions would continue proves to be false.

7   What is the object of an award of basic damages for breach of contract?

A   To ensure that the injured party receives payment for the acts performed.

B   To ensure that the injured party is in the same position as he would have been in had the contract been performed.

C   To ensure that the defaulting party does not profit from his breach.

D   To ensure that the defaulting party is penalised so that the breach will not recur.

8   Rodney and Horatio have entered into a contract whereby Rodney is to provide a ship to load waste at Palermo within 30 days of the ship's arrival. The ship arrives at Palermo but because the waste is unsafe, Horatio does not load it. The ship remains at Palermo but after 28 days the Italian government passes a law banning the transportation of unsafe waste by sea. The contract has been discharged by:

A   Anticipatory breach
B   Fundamental breach
C   Impossibility
D   Frustration

9   Emma was contracted to deliver two cases of champagne and 20 cases of wine from France to England for John's daughter's wedding. Emma was going to take the wine on the ferry while John flew back to England to carry on preparations that he was needed for there. Emma drove to Calais, but found that the ferry crossings had been cancelled due to high storms. She did not deliver the wine and the wedding guests had to drink water.

Emma claims that the contract was frustrated due to the cancellation of the ferry services because of the weather. What is the **correct** position?

A   Emma is right. The contract has been frustrated due to the weather preventing her completing her task.

B   Emma is wrong. The contract has not been frustrated by the weather, but by her inability to perform a personal service.

C   Emma is wrong. The contract has not been frustrated by the weather, but by the intervention of a third party, the ferry company.

D   Emma is wrong. The contract has not been frustrated at all. She could have carried out the delivery by an alternative route, such as the Channel tunnel.

10   Part payment of the contract price may not be recovered in exchange for incomplete performance where:

A   One party has prevented complete performance.
B   The work has been substantially completed.
C   Part of the work agreed under a fixed sum contract has been completed.
D   Part of the work agreed under a contract payable by instalment has been completed.

16 Contractual breakdown 3

1   Which of the following statements is/are **correct**?

    (i)   Specific performance is an order of the court directing a person to perform an obligation.
    (ii)   An order for specific performance will be made when the contract is for land.
    (iii)   An order for specific performance will not be made in a contract for personal services.

    A   (i) and (ii)
    B   (i) and (iii)
    C   (i), (ii) and (iii)
    D   None of the above

2   What must an injured party do when a contract is discharged by fundamental breach?

    A   He must either treat the contract as discharged or affirm it as still in force.
    B   He must treat the contract as discharged at once.
    C   He must continue with his own obligations if he wants to claim damages.
    D   He must seek an injunction if he wants to claim damages.

3   Which of the following is **not** a common law remedy?

    A   Damages
    B   Action for the price
    C   *Quantum meruit*
    D   Specific performance

4   A restitutory award which aims to restore the claimant to the position he would have been in but for the contract is known as:

    A   Mareva injunction
    B   *Restitutio in integrum*
    C   *Quantum meruit*
    D   Doctrine of laches

5   Harriet and Mark had entered into an agreement for the supply of goods to be delivered and paid for by instalments. Mark failed to pay the first instalment when it was due. Harriet refused to make further deliveries unless Mark paid cash on delivery. Mark refused to accept delivery on those terms. The price of the goods rose and Mark sued for breach of contract.

    Which of the following is **correct**?

    A   Harriet was entitled to repudiate when Mark failed to pay her the first instalment.

    B   Mark should have mitigated his loss by accepting the offer of delivery on cash payment terms.

    C   Damages will be based on the difference in the price of goods at the due date of delivery and the date of damages to account of the price rise.

    D   The contract has been frustrated by the price rise.

6   Robina agreed to write a book on Medieval Knights and Jousting for the History Alive Junior Series. She was to receive £4,000 on completion of the book. She had completed all the research and written a third of the book when History Alive decided to abandon the series.

What is Robina's legal position?

A   Robina has not discharged the contract by complete and exact performance, she will not be entitled to payment for what she has done.

B   Robina has only managed partial performance, she will only be entitled to payment for what she has done if History Alive accept partial performance.

C   Robina has been prevented from completing performance by History Alive. She is entitled to sue for damages or bring a quantum meruit action for the work she has done.

D   The contract has been frustrated by the abandonment of the series, Robina will not be entitled to payment for what she has done.

7   Vincent sells paintings by Pablo in his art shop. He has undertaken not to advertise the paintings at a lower price than Pablo has specified, only to sell the paintings to private collectors, and not to display any of Pablo's paintings without his permission. They have agreed that if Vincent breaks any of these conditions, he will have to pay Pablo £10,000.

Vincent hangs a picture that Pablo gave Vincent's wife for Christmas the previous year above the counter in his shop. Pablo claims that Vincent does not have permission to display the picture and is demanding £10,000.

A   Vincent owes Pablo £10,000 as liquidated damages.
B   Vincent owes Pablo £10,000 under a penalty clause.
C   Vincent owes Pablo nothing because the penalty clause is void.
D   Vincent may choose to not pay Pablo because the penalty clause is voidable.

8   Liquidated damages are:

A   Damages which have been paid out of a sum previously lodged with the court by the defendants.

B   A fixed or ascertainable sum agreed by the parties at the time of contracting payable in the event of a breach.

C   A sum of money payable under a contract in the event of a breach whose purpose is to deter a potential difficulty.

D   A measure of the value of contractual work done awarded to put the claimant in the position he would have been if the contract had never been performed.

9   Which of the following is **not** a genuine cause of a contract being frustrated?

A   Destruction of the subject matter
B   Non-occurrence of an event which is part of the purpose of the contract
C   Personal incapacity to perform a contract of personal service
D   Supervening illegality

10 Which of the following would cause a contract to be frustrated?

    A   An act beyond the control of the parties to the contract making the contract impossible to perform.

    B   A rise in the cost of raw materials making it impossible for one party to complete the contract at a profit.

    C   A large increase in orders making it impossible to deliver all the goods ordered by the date specified.

    D   An act by one of the parties to the contract making it impossible to perform.

17 Contractual breakdown 4

1   A contract may be discharged on the grounds of personal incapacity to perform a contract of personal service where:

    (i)   An employee's ill-health prevents him from performing his duties.

    (ii)   An employee dies.

    (iii)   An employee is sent to prison for six months.

    (iv)   An employee who is a foreign national is called up for military service.

    (v)   An employee is a national of a country on whom the UK declares war.

    A   (ii) only

    B   (i), (ii) and (iv) only

    C   (ii), (iii) and (v) only

    D   (i), (ii), (iii) and (iv) only

2   In damages for breach of contract, damages representing expectation interest are:

    A   Money to restore the claimant to the position that he would have been in if he had not relied on the contract.

    B   Money to put the claimant in the position that he would have been in if the contract had been properly performed.

    C   Interest charged on the sum of damages agreed between the date of breach of contract and the date of payment.

    D   Interest charged to cover the effects of inflation since the breach.

3   Davina engages Rupert as interior decorator and designer to do up her flat in South Kensington. The contract is for a fixed sum of £7,500. Within the allotted time Rupert informs Davina that the work is completed. On inspection Davina finds that the doorbell does not chime and an aspidistra she requested has not been supplied. Must she pay Rupert?

    A   Yes: though she may retain the purchase price of the aspidistra and amount for repair of the chimes.

    B   Yes: the contract has been substantially performed and the full £7,500 must be paid.

    C   No: the failures in performance constitute anticipatory breach.

    D   No: performance must be complete, entire and exact so nothing is payable until the defects are put right.

4   Whin Mechanics Ltd agree to service a fleet of trucks for Rigg Enterprises Ltd for a total price of £20,000. Work is agreed to commence on 1 June and to be completed by 15 June. Owing to a strike and to problems with spare parts, the service of all the trucks is only completed on 30 June. Whin Mechanics Ltd admit to breach of contract but dispute the amount of damages claimed, being £10,000 for loss of half a month's business profits (as certified by the auditors) £20,000 for the loss of certified profits on a highly lucrative new contract which was offered to the company on 20 June but which could not be taken up.

How much will Whin Mechanics Ltd have to pay?

A   Nothing. The losses are too remote.

B   £10,000. Only normal business profits are recoverable.

C   £20,000. Whin should have anticipated the special contract.

D   £30,000. Normal business profits are recoverable and it is foreseeable that a severe delay will lose a customer profits which may become available.

5   Betty runs a farm where she breeds dogs. She contracted with Seth to build a walk in refrigerator where all the food for the dogs would be kept. Seth built the refrigerator wrongly and all the dog food Betty put in there went mouldy. Betty did not realise that the food had gone bad and fed it to the dogs. All the dogs suffered stomach problems for a few days. One dog, a rare breed, developed an acute case of food poisoning and died.

Betty is claiming damages for the value of the dead dog and also loss of profits from selling the dog when it was more mature. Will she succeed?

A   No. The death of one of Betty's dogs as a result of an error in the refrigerator could not have been within Seth's contemplation.

B   Yes. But Seth is liable for the value of the dead dog only. It is unclear what profits would have arisen from the sale of the dog.

C   Yes. But Seth is liable for the value of a standard dead dog only. He could not have known that a rare dog would die.

D   Yes. Seth is liable for serious consequences, as food poisoning is not too remote to have been within his contemplation and he was working for a dog breeder, who was likely to own valuable dogs.

6   In which of the following circumstances will a decree for specific performance **not** be available?

A   In a contract for the sale of land
B   In a contract made by deed for land
C   In a contract of employment
D   In a contract to pay money to a third party

7   Belinda engaged Botch Job Bathrooms to install a bathroom on the first floor of her house. The price of the job was £7,500 and it included converting the old bathroom into a study. On completion of the job, she discovered that the plumbing in the old bathroom had not been correctly removed and that there was a leak in the wall behind her bookshelves. The new bathroom is fine. She was forced to bring someone in to correct the plumbing in her study at a cost of £500. She is refusing to pay Botch Job Bathrooms.

What is the legal position?

A   The contract has been completed and Belinda must pay Botch Job Bathrooms.

B   Belinda has prevented Botch Job Bathrooms from completing performance by getting another plumber in. Therefore she must pay the full sum.

C   The contract was performed in a seriously substandard fashion and Belinda does not have to pay for it.

D   The contract has been substantially performed and Belinda must pay Botch Job Bathrooms £7,500 less the cost of righting the problems, that is £7,000.

8   Which of the following is **not** a reasonable ground for frustration of a contract?

A   The destruction by lightning of a hall let out for a concert.

B   The onset of illness in the lead singer of a pop group.

C   An outbreak of war, causing a ship to be trapped in a port until the end of hostilities.

D   The closure due to bad weather of a mountain pass, causing traffic to take an alternative route, 300 miles longer.

9   Tee Ltd contracted with Vee Ltd to deliver goods to Vee Ltd to the value of £5,000. Vee Ltd accepted the goods but the amount due remains outstanding. Tee Ltd may:

A   Recover damages for breach of contract subject to its obligation to take reasonable steps to mitigate its loss.

B   Apply for an order of specific performance to force Vee Ltd to pay.

C   Sue for the price without any obligation to mitigate.

D   Take back the goods that have been delivered to Vee Ltd.

10   Sarah owes her friend, Sally-Anne, £100. Sally-Anne agrees to waive her right to the debt if Sarah, who is a dressmaker, makes her a dress to wear to a ball that she has been invited to at college. Sarah makes the dress and gives it to Sally-Anne. Unfortunately, the ball is cancelled and Sally-Anne has no need for the dress. She returns the dress to Sarah, assuming it can be sold in the shop, and asks for payment of the £100 instead.

What is the legal position?

A   Sally-Anne is entitled to £100 under the original agreement.

B   Sally-Anne is not entitled to £100 as she has waived her right to the money and accepted a dress in its place.

C   Sally-Anne is entitled to the £100 as the dress is not as valuable as the £100 so the second promise has insufficient consideration.

D   Sally-Anne is entitled to the £100 as she would have had to pay for the dress, as dressmaking is Sarah's business.

18 Employment 1

1   An employer always has a duty to:

    A   Provide facilities for smokers
    B   Give employees who leave a reference
    C   Provide work
    D   Behave reasonably and responsibly toward employees

2   As a general rule, in relation to a claim for unfair dismissal, which three of the following statements are **incorrect**?

    ☐   Employees of any age may be eligible to claim
    ☐   There is no qualifying period
    ☐   There is frequently no limit on the amount of compensation that a tribunal can award
    ☐   Claims must be made within three months of the dismissal
    ☐   Employees taking part in unofficial strike action are protected from unfair dismissal

3   An inspector has wide powers which may be used against an employer who contravenes health and safety requirements. Which of the following is **not** available to him?

    A   A criminal prosecution
    B   A prohibition notice
    C   An improvement notice
    D   A civil action for damages

4   Which of the following reasons is **not** valid for the dismissal of an employee?

    A   Dishonesty
    B   Wilful disobedience of a lawful order
    C   Membership of a trade union
    D   Misconduct

5   Mick has been employed by Deck Line Ltd for four years. He was aware that the company was experiencing trading difficulties but is still shocked to be sent home without notice when Deck Line Ltd is compulsorily wound up. He sues for wrongful dismissal but at the hearing the liquidator proves that he has discovered that Mick has embezzled £20,000 from the company. Will Mick succeed in his claim?

    A   Yes. He has been constructively dismissed.

    B   Yes. He has been wrongfully dismissed without notice and no regard should be paid to the embezzlement discovered later.

    C   No. The employment contract was frustrated by Deck Line Ltd's liquidation.

    D   No. Deck Line Ltd was justified in its dismissal of Mick.

6   Miranda works for Little Company. The Big Company plc buys Little Company. Under the TUPE regulations, Miranda has the right to:

     A   Resign and claim unfair dismissal.

     B   Recover redundancy pay if she chooses to leave her employment.

     C   Carry forward her period of employment with Little Company as continuous employment.

     D   Demand an employment contract under exactly the same terms as with Little Company, regardless of any organisational reasons for the contrary.

7   In which of the following situations has there been no dismissal?

     A   An employer asks an employee to leave his premises and never to return.

     B   An employer completely changes the nature of an employee's job, as a result of which, she resigns.

     C   An employment contract is frustrated by reason of the employee being in prison.

     D   A fixed term contract expires and is not renewed.

8   In which of the following areas is an employee not protected by legislation?

     A   Dismissal on grounds of competence

     B   Dismissal on grounds of race

     C   Dismissal on grounds of disability

     D   Dismissal on grounds of sex

9   Claire's employment with Wye Ltd began 8 years ago. Her contract of employment states that she may be required to work at any of the company's offices in London, Birmingham or Manchester. Claire has for the entire 8 years worked at the company's London office. The company has now asked Claire to move to its Manchester office.

     Which of the following statements is **correct**?

     A   Claire cannot be required to move to the Manchester office.

     B   Claire's contract contains a mobility clause which permits her employer to require her to work at any of the company's offices.

     C   The fact that Claire has always worked in the London office prohibits her employer from requiring her to move to any of the company's other offices.

     D   If Claire is required to move to the Manchester office, she may make a claim for automatic unfair and wrongful dismissal.

10   H plc carries on its business using both employees and independent contractors. It is important for H plc to be able to distinguish between its employees and independent contractors for a number of reasons.

     Which of the following is **incorrect**?

     A   Employees have a right not to be unfairly dismissed but this does not apply to independent contractors.

     B   H plc must deduct income tax and national insurance contributions from the wages paid to its employees, but not from the amount paid to independent contractors.

     C   Both employees and independent contractors can enforce contractual rights against H plc.

     D   Both employees and independent contractors would rank as preferential creditors in respect of unpaid wages, if H plc went into insolvent liquidation.

19 Employment 2

1   The employment tribunal has just established that Ken was unfairly dismissed. There has been a breakdown of confidence between Ken and his former employers. The tribunal is likely to rule for:

A   Reinstatement
B   Re-engagement
C   Compensation
D   A punitive additional award

2   Which of the following statements is/are **correct**?

(i)   The most common remedy for wrongful dismissal is damages. The measure of damages is usually the sum that would have been earned if proper notice had been given.

(ii) Where breach of contract leaves the employer as the injured party, he may dismiss the employee and withhold wages.

A   (i) only
B   (ii) only
C   Both (i) and (ii)
D   Neither (i) nor (ii)

3   Which of the following tests is not an accepted test applied by the courts to determine whether a person is an employee or an independent sub-contractor?

A   The control test
B   The documentation test
C   The integration test
D   The multiple (economic reality) test

4   Pretty Plastics Ltd is a factory that takes raw materials and produces a range of plastic sheeting.

One day, a large amount of oil flooded an area of the yard outside. Sawdust was laid down, but a small patch was left uncovered when the sawdust ran out. Employees were warned of the dangers. An employee, Josh, slipped and injured his back. Is Pretty Plastics liable for damages?

A   No, it took all reasonable steps to prevent the accident.
B   No, as Josh was negligent.
C   Yes, as employers have a duty to prevent accidents.
D   Yes, as the company should have foreseen the accident and prevented it.

5   An employee has been continuously employed for one and a half years. He is entitled to:

A   Three months' notice
B   A minimum of a week's notice
C   One week's notice for every year of his employment (ie one and a half weeks' notice)
D   A month's notice

6   Which of the following is **not** one of the reasons that the distinction between employees and the independent sub-contractors is important?

A   Employers must withhold income tax on independent sub-contractors' pay.

B   There is significant employment legislation which confers benefit and protection on employees.

C   Independent contractors are treated as non-preferential creditors in the event of the company being wound up.

D   Employers are generally vicariously liable for the tortious acts of employees during the course of employment. Liability is severely restricted in the case of independent sub-contractors.

7   Which of the following statements is/are **correct**?

(i)   An employer always has a duty to provide work for his employees.
(ii)   An employer has a duty to give a reference if an employee leaves to take up another job.

A   (i) only
B   (ii) only
C   Both (i) and (ii)
D   Neither (i) nor (ii)

8   In which of the following situations is being male **not** considered a genuine occupational qualification?

A   A job abroad in a country whose laws and customs might make it difficult for a woman to perform her duties.

B   A job in parts of the UK where custom might make it difficult for a woman to perform her duties.

C   A job as the attendant in a male lavatory.

D   A job as a minister of religion.

9   Which of the following is **not** a duty of the employer?

A   To allow an employee time off for ante-natal care.
B   To provide an itemised pay slip (to those working more than eight hours a week).
C   To provide references for the employee when the employee seeks other employment.
D   To take reasonable care of employees.

10   Which of the following is **not** a genuine rule for calculating length of service?

A   A week is a week in which the employee is employed for at least eight hours under a contract for employment for eight hours or more.

B   Maternity leave is included in reckoning continuity and length of service.

C   If an employee works for the required number of hours under separate contracts for an employer he may aggregate the hours.

D   Service of an employee of a business is carried forward if the business is transferred to another organisation.

20 Employment 3

1   Which of the following statements is **correct**?

    A   A director cannot also be an employee of the company.
    B   A shareholder cannot also be an employee of the company.
    C   A partner cannot also be an employee of the firm.
    D   A lender cannot also be an employee of the firm.

2   Which of the following is/are sources of terms of a contract of employment?

    (i)   Custom and practice
    (ii)   A collective agreement between the union and the employer

    A   (i) only
    B   (ii) only
    C   Both (i) and (ii)
    D   Neither (i) nor (ii)

3   An employee is always entitled to:

    A   Patent rights on any invention produced by the employee at the workplace.
    B   Use confidential information after the employment has ceased.
    C   Require his employer to give a reference if other work is being sought.
    D   Disobey an order from his employer if it is unreasonable.

4   Claims for both common law damages for wrongful dismissal and statutory compensation for unfair dismissal may be heard by

    (i)   The courts
    (ii)   Employment tribunals

    Which of the above is/are **correct**?

    A   (i) only
    B   (ii) only
    C   Both (i) and (ii)
    D   Neither (i) nor (ii)

5   An employer must allow an employee time off work:

    A   For trade union duties
    B   To attend an interview for another job
    C   To attend a course of training
    D   To attend the funeral of a close relative

6   Which of the following might **not** be termination of employment by an employer's breach of contract?

    A   Summary dismissal
    B   Constructive dismissal
    C   Wrongful dismissal
    D   Inability on the employer's behalf to continue

7   Which of the following statements suggests that John is an independent contractor in relation to the work he carries out for Zed Ltd?

    (i)   He is required to provide his own tools.

    (ii)   He is required to carry out his work personally and is not free to send a substitute.

    (iii)   He is paid in full without any deduction of income tax.

    A   (i) and (ii) only

    B   (i) and (iii) only

    C   (ii) and (iii) only

    D   All of the above

8   An employer will be vicariously liable for the act of an employee where:

    (i)   There is an employer/employee relationship

    (ii)   The act is criminal only

    (iii)   The act is committed in the course of employment

    (iv)   The act is an independent act of the employee

    A   (i) and (ii) only

    B   (i) and (iii) only

    C   (i), (ii) and (iii) only

    D   (ii), (iii) and (iv) only

9   Which of the following is **not** normally implied into a contract of employment by the common law?

    A   A duty to provide a reference

    B   A duty to provide work

    C   A duty to pay reasonable remuneration

    D   An employee's duty to obey lawful instructions

10   Which of the following is **not** a potentially fair reason for dismissal?

    A   Membership of a trade union

    B   Taking part in strike action

    C   Being a threat to national security

    D   Legal prohibition, such as a van driver losing his driving licence

21 Employment 4

1   Which of the following groups are not excluded from the statutory unfair dismissal code?

    A   Armed forces

    B   Person ordinarily employed outside Great Britain

    C   Ministers of religion

    D   Employees dismissed while taking unofficial strike action

2   Where must a claim for wrongful dismissal be brought?

A   The Employment Tribunal only
B   The County Court only
C   The High Court only
D   The County Court, the High Court or the Employment Tribunal

3   Which of the following is **not** a duty of the employee?

A   Reasonable competence
B   Obedience to instructions (unless required act is unlawful or will expose employee to personal danger)
C   Absence of error in work undertaken
D   Personal service

4   Which of the following is **not** an example of lawful racial discrimination?

A   To help a new employee integrate into the organisation
B   To add to authenticity in art
C   To add to the authenticity of a restaurant
D   To provide personal welfare services

5   An employer must give an employee a statement of prescribed particulars of his employment within two months of the beginning of their contract. Which of the following is **not** required to be part of that statement?

A   The names of the employer and the employee
B   The rules on health and safety in the workplace
C   Length of termination notice required on either side
D   Whether any service with a previous employer forms part of the employee's period of employment

6   Vicki has been employed by Ringview Ltd for ten years. What is the minimum notice to which she is entitled?

A   One month
B   Five weeks
C   Ten weeks
D   Twelve weeks

7   In which of the following situations is the employee **not** automatically entitled to time off work?

A   To receive ante-natal care.

B   To attend job interviews, having resigned from his position.

C   To attend trade union branch meetings, provided that it is a recognised, independent union and the employee is a member.

D   To attend job interviews, having been made redundant.

8   Which of the following reasons justify dismissal as fair?

(i)   An auditor employed by an auditing firm is struck off their professional body's list for malpractice.

(ii)   A person employed as finance director and claiming to be a qualified accountant only has a maths GCSE in fact.

(iii)   A nuclear scientist, despite frequent warnings, persistently fails to secure his experiments, thereby causing danger to colleagues.

(iv)   A solicitor's contract with a firm of solicitors is not renewed because the partners plan to windup the firm.

A   (i) and (ii) only
B   (iii) and (iv) only
C   (i), (ii) and (iii) only
D   All of the above

9   Kay Michael Ltd operates a chemical processing plant at which it employs Roger. Although statute recommends their use, safety goggles are only kept in a locker in the canteen and there are instructions to use them posted at head office. The foreman discourages their use since they slow down work and so decrease the amount of productivity bonus which he earns. When Roger requests a pair therefore he is persuaded that he does not need them. There is an accident and Roger is blinded, but he can prove that had he worn goggles he would have been uninjured. What is Kay Michael Ltd's position?

(i)   It is liable to Roger for breach of statutory duty
(ii)   It is open to the company to raise the defence that it took reasonable care to ensure Roger's safety
(iii)   It can raise the defence of consent against Roger
(iv)   It is liable to Roger at common law for failure to provide a safe system of work

A   (i) and (iii) only
B   (ii) and (iv) only
C   (i), (iii) and (iv) only
D   All of the above

10   Nick commences employment under a three-year contract with Adieu Ltd on 1.8.X6. On 30.6.X9 he is given notice that the contract is not to be renewed. Assuming that he has a case, what claims may he bring against Adieu Ltd?

A   Wrongful dismissal only
B   Unfair dismissal only
C   Redundancy only
D   Redundancy and unfair dismissal only

22 Company formation 1

1   Which **three** of the following are **correct**?

A private company limited by shares:

☐ Cannot offer its shares or debentures to the public

☐ Cannot allow its shareholders to offer their shares direct to the public

☐ Must have a minimum of two members, otherwise the sole member may become personally liable for the debts of the company

☐ Cannot be registered with a name which is the same as that of an existing registered company

☐ Must have at least two directors

2   In relation to a company's articles of association, which of the following is **incorrect**?

A   The articles of association set down the internal regulations of a company.

B   Promoters may or may not submit their own form of articles when submitting the forms necessary to form a company limited by shares.

C   The articles of association form a contract between the members and the company and the members amongst themselves.

D   Any article of association may be changed by special resolution, subject to the right of the holders of 15% of the company's shares or debentures to object to the court.

3   Before being permitted to trade, a public company must have:

A   Obtained a Certificate of Incorporation only
B   Been listed on the London Stock Exchange
C   Obtained a Trading Certificate and Certificate of Incorporation
D   Issued a prospectus

4   What type of resolution is required to alter a company's name?

A   Special resolution
B   Ordinary resolution
C   Ordinary resolution with special notice
D   Special resolution with special notice

5   A public company limited by shares must have:

A   At least two directors, and one shareholder
B   At least one director, one company secretary and two shareholders
C   At least two directors, one company secretary and two shareholders
D   At least two directors, one company secretary and one shareholder

6   If a contract is entered into by promoters before the incorporation of a company, which of the following is **incorrect**?

    A   The company may ratify the contract as soon as it receives its certificate of incorporation.

    B   Subject to agreement to the contrary, the promoters may be held personally liable on the contract.

    C   The company cannot enforce the contract prior to its incorporation.

    D   The company cannot be held liable even if it has adopted the contract after receiving its certificate of incorporation.

7   Which of the following companies would **not** be permitted to omit the word limited or Ltd at the end of its name?

    A   Art for All Limited, whose object it is to bring art exhibitions to the deprived inner cities.

    B   Nigel's Nails Limited, whose object is the establishment of a chain of nail bars throughout the UK.

    C   The Lawyers' Information Service Limited, whose object is to encourage the distribution of information to students about the legal profession.

    D   Science for Schools Limited, whose object is to raise funds to supply scientific instruments for schools.

8   Which **three** of the following documents must be submitted to register a company limited by shares?

☐ A memorandum of association

☐ Articles of association

☐ A statement of the first directors and secretary

☐ A statutory declaration of compliance with the requirements of the Companies Act

☐ A register of members

9   If a company's actions are restricted by its objects, which of the following is **correct**?

    A   Ultra vires contracts with third parties are invalid.

    B   Ultra vires contracts with third parties are valid.

    C   Ultra vires contracts with third parties are valid only if the third party enquired into the existence of any limitations.

    D   Ultra vires contracts with third parties are valid even in the event of lack of good faith being proved against the third party.

10   The articles of association of a company limited by shares form a contract between:

    A   The shareholders and the company in all respects

    B   The shareholders and the directors in all respects

    C   The company and the directors in respect of directors' rights only

    D   The company and the shareholders in respect of shareholder rights only

23 Company formation 2

1   Tom has transferred his business to Tom Ltd, a company limited by shares. Which of the following statements is **correct**?

   A   Tom Ltd is fully liable for all debts and liabilities of the business incurred after the date of transfer.

   B   Tom is fully liable for all debts and liabilities of the business incurred after the date of transfer.

   C   Tom and Tom Ltd are jointly liable for all debts and liabilities of the business incurred after the date of transfer.

   D   Tom Ltd and its shareholders are fully liable for all debts and liabilities incurred after the date of transfer.

2   Which three of the following records must be kept and made available for inspection by the members?

   ☐   The register of directors' residential addresses
   ☐   The register of members
   ☐   Copies of directors' service contracts
   ☐   The register of debentureholders
   ☐   Register of charges

3   Which of the following is **not** an example of an artificial legal person?

   A   A company limited by guarantee
   B   A private company with only one member
   C   A partner in a partnership
   D   A corporation sole

4   Which of the following statements are true or false?

Statement	True	False
A director's service address can be the company's registered office.		
Directors' service contracts must be made available for inspection by the general public.		
The register of members contains among other things the name and address of each member.		
A company does not legally have to keep a register of debentureholders.		

5   Sally and Petra run a business jointly. They each have £5,000 of capital in the business and decide to form a registered company in which they will be the sole shareholders. What type of company should they form if they wish to protect their other assets?

   A   A private company limited by shares
   B   A public company limited by shares
   C   A private company limited by guarantee
   D   An unlimited private company

6　Which **three** of the following are requirements of Limited Liability Partnerships (LLPs)?

☐　Sign and file accounts
☐　Appoint auditors if appropriate
☐　Notify the Registrar of any qualifications held by the members
☐　Notify the Registrar when a member leaves
☐　Submit a copy of the partnership agreement to the Registrar

7　Any alteration of a company's articles must:

A　Benefit the shareholders concerned
B　Benefit the company as a whole
C　Benefit the directors
D　Be approved by the Court

8　How can a promoter ensure that the expenses they incur in setting up a company will be recoverable?

A　By making it clear in all transactions that they are acting as agent for the company.

B　By entering into a contract with the company after its incorporation for reimbursement of expenses by the company.

C　They have no automatic right, but by drafting the articles of the company, they can provide for the reimbursement of expenses.

D　By declaring in all transactions that they are a trustee for the company.

9　Joe owns a newsagent, runs it as manager and employs Jess as part-time help during the week. He is fully liable for the business' debts. What type of business does Joe own?

A　A partnership
B　A company limited by guarantee
C　A sole trader
D　A limited company

10　Which of the following changes must always be made to an off-the-shelf company when it is purchased from a formation agent?

A　Changing its register of members
B　Restricting its objects
C　Changing its articles
D　Changing its name

24 Company formation 3

1   A public limited company cannot commence business or borrow money until the nominal value of the company's allotted share capital is not less than:

    A   £12,500
    B   £25,000
    C   £40,000
    D   £50,000

2   The case of *Salomon v Salomon 1897* confirmed which important principle of company law?

    A   A company and its members are separate legal persons.

    B   A director cannot take a decision to employ himself and later make a claim against the company as an employee.

    C   When a company is wound up, directors who knowingly carried on the business with intent to defraud creditors may be made personally liable for the company's liabilities.

    D   The sale of a business to a company owned by the vendor of the business will be a legal nullity if the sale made no change in the business's commercial position.

3   Within what period of time after the year end must a company file its accounts with the Registrar?

    A   Three months for a public company and six months for a private company
    B   Nine months for a public company and seven months for a private company
    C   Six months for a public company and nine months for a private company
    D   Ten months for a public company and twelve months for a private company

4   How can a company restrict its objects?

    A   By ordinary resolution
    B   By special resolution
    C   By extraordinary resolution
    D   It cannot restrict its objects

5   To what extent is a member of a company limited by guarantee personally liable to contribute towards the company's debts?

    A   He is liable to contribute towards all the company's debts at any time.
    B   He is liable for all the company's debts on a winding up only.
    C   His liability to contribute is limited to the amount he agreed to upon a winding up.
    D   His liability to contribute is limited to the amount he agreed to at any time.

6   Five brothers own and are directors of a limited company that carries on the family business. They are thinking of changing it to an unlimited partnership.

Which **three** features of the business would not be affected by this change?

☐ The ability to sue in the business's name

☐ The ability to mortgage the business's assets

☐ The treatment of the brothers' income from the business for tax purposes

☐ The ability to create a floating charge over the business's assets

☐ The brothers' rights to participate in the management of the business

---

7   Joe and Ken have applied to have Weston Ltd registered as a private limited company limited by shares, but have failed to submit any articles of association. What effect will this have on their application?

A   The Registrar will refuse to register the company.

B   Model articles will automatically apply to the company.

C   The company will be provisionally registered and the articles will be determined at the first meeting of the shareholders.

D   The company will be provisionally registered but may not trade until articles are submitted.

---

8   What is the significance of a company's unrestricted objects?

A   It is virtually impossible for a company to enter into an *ultra vires* commercial contract.

B   All contracts with third parties will be enforceable.

C   The company must seek authority from the members to enter into all contracts.

D   Shareholders cannot prevent a company entering any contracts.

---

9   In Paul Ltd's articles there is a clause stating that Fred should act as solicitor to the company for life. A number of members are unhappy with Fred's performance and have sufficient votes to change the articles to remove him from office. Are they able to do this?

A   Yes, and Fred has no recourse against the company.

B   Yes, but Fred can sue the company for breach of contract.

C   No, because the articles cannot be changed for this reason.

D   No, because the articles cannot be changed to override the contract with Fred.

---

10   Which **three** of the following are characteristics of a partnership?

☐ There are at least two partners.

☐ There must be an intention to trade.

☐ There must be some form of business activity.

☐ Partners are agents of the partnership.

☐ Partners are only liable for contracts they personally signed.

25 Company formation 4

1   A private company limited by shares must be registered with:

   A   At least one member, who may also be the sole director and company secretary

   B   At least one member, who may also be the sole director; no company secretary is required

   C   At least one member, who cannot also act as a director or company secretary

   D   At least two members, one of whom may act as a director and the other as company secretary

2   Paul, a promoter, is in the process of incorporating Vendor Ltd, and has ordered goods to be used by the company. He has signed the order form 'Paul, for and on behalf of Vendor Ltd'. Who is liable if the goods are not paid for?

   A   Vendor Ltd

   B   Paul

   C   Paul and Vendor Ltd jointly

   D   Neither Paul nor Vendor Ltd as there is no contract

3   Mr X owns shares in Y Ltd. This means that Mr X

   (i)   Is a part-owner of Y Ltd

   (ii)   Is a part-owner of Y Ltd's property

   Which of the above is/are **correct**?

   A   (i) only

   B   (ii) only

   C   Both (i) and (ii)

   D   Neither (i) nor (ii)

4   Which of the following is **not** a situation in which the court will 'lift the veil of incorporation'?

   A   Where the members or directors are using the veil to evade their legal obligations.

   B   Where the directors are in breach of the regulations governing the giving of financial assistance for the purchase of the company's own shares.

   C   Where the corporate structure is being used as a sham.

   D   Where it is in the public interest.

5   All the following statements relate to a company's articles of association.

Are they true or false?

Statement	True	False
The articles of association sets out the regulations governing the internal conduct of the company.		
The articles of association are registered with the registrar of companies after the registrar has issued a certificate of incorporation.		
The articles of association are required for a public company, but not for a private company.		
The articles of association must state the company's name.		

6   What is an *ultra vires* action?

    A   An illegal act for which a company cannot be given capacity

    B   An act contrary to the company's mission statement

    C   An act beyond the company's capacity to contract

    D   An act which is beyond the established commercial activities of the company

7   Which **three** of the following must be sent to the Registrar when forming a limited liability partnership (LLP)?

- [ ] A £20 registration fee.
- [ ] The registered office address.
- [ ] The name of the LLP.
- [ ] The names and addresses of all the members.
- [ ] A copy of the partnership agreement.

8   Crawley Ltd, a newly created private company, agreed to buy a valuable antique for £10,000 from Charles, one of its promoters, before issuing a prospectus which does not disclose the transaction. The antique is only worth £7,500, but the company have already entered into a contract to sell it on to Broadfield Ltd for £12,500. What action should Crawley Ltd take against Charles?

    A   Rescind the contract

    B   Pay Charles the cost price of £7,500 only

    C   Sue Charles for £2,500

    D   Nothing

9   Which of the following authorised and issued share capitals would meet the requirements for a private limited company re-registering as a public limited company?

    A   30,000 shares with a nominal value of £1 (75p paid)

    B   40,000 shares with a nominal value of £1 (fully paid)

    C   50,000 shares with a nominal value of £1 (35p paid)

    D   80,000 shares with a nominal value of £1 (20p paid)

10   What is the minimum percentage of the nominal value of the company's issued share capital that a member or members must hold in order to initiate proceedings to have an alteration of the articles concerning their class rights cancelled?

A   5%
B   10%
C   15%
D   20%

26 Company formation 5

1   Which of the following statements are true or false concerning the alteration of articles of association?

Statement	True	False
Alterations may compel a member to subscribe for additional shares.		
Alterations are void if they conflict with the Companies Act.		
A person cannot obtain an injunction to prevent the alteration of articles where the alteration affects their contract contained within it.		
An alteration may be deemed void if it can be proved that the majority who passed it were not acting bona fide in the interests of the company as a whole.		

2   Tunnel Ltd has passed a special resolution to alter its articles of association, to allow the compulsory transfer to the directors of the shares of any member competing with the company's business. A minority of the shareholders are in a competing business, and are seeking to have this alteration declared invalid, in view of the hardship to them as minority shareholders. What is the position?

A   The alteration is valid if it is passed bona fide for the best interests of the company as a whole.

B   The alteration is invalid, since it constitutes a fraud on the minority.

C   The alteration is valid, irrespective of the motives behind it, since a company has an inherent right to alter its articles.

D   The resolution is invalid, since it contravenes statutory rights given to all members.

3   Wilde Ltd is a new company. Its finance director asks you how long it should keep accounting records for to comply with the Companies Act. Your reply is:

A   3 years
B   6 years
C   9 years
D   12 years

4   Which **three** of the following are differences between a public and private company?

☐   A public company has six months from the end of its accounting period to produce and file its annual accounts; a private company has nine months.

☐   A company limited by guarantee can only be a private company; it cannot be a public company.

☐   The Companies Act rule that ordinary shares allotted for cash must be first offered to members applies to public, not private, companies.

☐   Under the Companies Act, private companies do not have to hold an AGM.

☐   A private company must have at least one member, public companies must have two.

---

5   How long after the anniversary date does a company have to file its next annual return?

A   7 days
B   14 days
C   21 days
D   28 days

---

6   Which remedy for a passing-off action prevents a company from using another's registered name?

A   Restitution
B   Damages
C   Injunction
D   Specific performance

---

7   What is the legal position if a company enters into an *ultra vires* contract with one of its directors?

A   The contract is void.
B   The contract is void unless undertaken in good faith by the director.
C   The director has breached his duty to abide by the company's constitution.
D   The contract is valid, and cannot be retracted by the company.

---

8   Which of the following does **not** always apply to optional additional clauses inserted in a company's articles?

A   Clauses can be entrenched by providing special conditions that must be met before they can be altered.

B   Clauses can give a member power by requiring their presence at a meeting for a quorum to be present.

C   No alteration of the memorandum can compel a member to subscribe for additional shares.

D   If the clause relates to class rights, these can be altered by a special resolution.

---

9   A company's constitution binds which of the following?

(i)   The company
(ii)   Members
(iii)   Third parties

A   (i) and (ii) only
B   (i) and (iii) only
C   (ii) and (iii) only
D   All of the above

10   Jake, the promoter of Peg Ltd, decided to set up the company on 20 January 20X9. He sent the required documents to Companies House on 20 February 20X9. On 26 February 20X9 he rang Companies House to find out when the company will be incorporated, he was told the 27 February 20X9. When the Certificate of Incorporation arrived, the incorporation date is 1 March 20X9. When was the company formed?

A   20 January 20X9
B   20 February 20X9
C   27 February 20X9
D   1 March 20X9

27 Company formation 6

1   Are the following statements true or false about a private limited company?

Statement	True	False
A private limited company is a company which has not registered under the Companies Act to be a public company.		
A private limited company is an incorporated business.		
A private limited company is not required by law to file annual accounts at Companies House.		
The shareholders of a private company cannot benefit from limited liability.		

2   Which of the following are prohibited activities for public companies until a trading certificate has been acquired?

A   Trading only
B   Borrowing only
C   Listing on a stock exchange only
D   All of the above

3   Lynn runs a florist shop. The name of the business is Lynn (Flowers) Ltd. From this information you can infer

A   Lynn (Flowers) Ltd is a private company.
B   Lynn (Flowers) Ltd is a public company.
C   Lynn is a sole trader.
D   Lynn has unlimited liability for the business's debts.

4   The publication used by the Registrar of Companies to publish certain legal notices is called:

   A   London Gazette
   B   London Times
   C   London Law
   D   London Standard

5   Ton Ltd is a wholly-owned subsidiary of MBI plc. Fred supplied goods on credit to Ton Ltd, knowing that it was part of the prosperous MBI group. Ton Ltd ran into trading difficulties and is now insolvent. Fred's legal remedy for recovery of his unpaid debt lies against:

   A   MBI plc
   B   The directors of Ton Ltd
   C   The directors of MBI Ltd
   D   Ton Ltd

6   Alf and Bert decided to form a company. On 25 April 20X6 they sent the necessary documents to the Registrar. On 10 June 20X6 they received the certificate of incorporation dated 1 May 20X6. Subsequently they discovered that the company was registered on 1 June 20X6.

   What was the date of incorporation?

   A   1 March 20X6
   B   1 May 20X6
   C   10 May 20X6
   D   1 June 20X6

7   Which **three** of the following statements are advantages of operating as a sole trader?

   ☐   No requirement to file accounts
   ☐   All the profit accrues to the owner
   ☐   The business is liable for all business debts
   ☐   More control over the business than a company
   ☐   Easier to raise finance

8   Krystle was formerly employed by Dynasty Ltd. She has entered into a covenant not to compete with Dynasty Ltd. The covenant is reasonable and not in restraint of trade. Krystle has formed a company, Krystle (Services) Ltd, which has started to trade in competition with Dynasty Ltd. Will Dynasty Ltd be able to get an injunction to prevent Krystle (Services) Ltd from trading?

   A   No, because Krystle (Services) Ltd has a separate legal identity.
   B   Yes, because the company has been formed as a device to mask Krystle's carrying on of the trade.
   C   No, because a company is not liable for the actions of its shareholders.
   D   Yes, because Krystle (Services) Ltd is engaging in fraudulent trading.

9   Model articles apply automatically, unless they are excluded or modified when the company is registered in the case of:

A   Private companies only

B   Public companies only

C   Companies limited by guarantee only

D   All companies limited by shares

---

10   Which of the following are statutory grounds for lifting the veil of incorporation?

(i)   A public company failing to obtain a trading certificate.

(ii)   Fraudulent or wrongful trading.

(iii)   The director of a company that has gone into liquidation becoming a director of a new company with an identical or very similar name to the liquidated company.

(iv)   A listed company carrying on business contrary to the Combined Code.

A   (i) and (iii) only

B   (ii) and (iv) only

C   (i), (ii) and (iii) only

D   (i), (ii) and (iv) only

---

28 Company administration and management 1

1   Which of the following is **incorrect**?

A   Directors are agents of a company.

B   If the board of directors exceeds its powers, the company cannot be held liable on a contract with a third party.

C   Individual directors are not permitted to contract on behalf of the company unless authorised by the company.

D   The board of directors may delegate authority to a managing director who may contract on behalf of the company.

---

2   To dismiss a director under s 168 Companies Act 2006 requires:

A   An ordinary resolution with 14 days' notice to the company

B   A special resolution with 14 days' notice to the company

C   An ordinary resolution with 28 days' notice to the company

D   A special resolution with 28 days' notice to the company

---

3   To enable a public company to call a general meeting by giving 'short notice':

A   Shareholders holding not less than 95% of all the company's shares must agree.

B   Shareholders holding 95% of the shares represented at the meeting must agree.

C   95% of all the shareholders must agree.

D   95% of all the shareholders present at the meeting must agree.

4   Which of the following **cannot** be achieved by ordinary resolution?

A   The approval of company accounts
B   The dismissal of a director
C   An alteration of a company's articles of association
D   The dismissal of an auditor

5   In relation to the company secretary, which of the following is **correct**?

A   A company secretary of a private or public company is not required to be appropriately qualified.

B   A public company need not appoint a person to be company secretary.

C   A company secretary cannot bind the company in contract.

D   A company secretary cannot bind the company in contract if acting outside their actual or apparent authority.

6   Which **three** of the following can be carried out by written resolution of a private company?

☐   The alteration of the articles of association
☐   The appointment of a director
☐   The removal of an auditor
☐   Reduction of share capital
☐   The removal of a director

7   Which **three** of the following are situations in which a meeting may be validly held that is only attended by one person?

☐   Where the articles provide a quorum of one for a general meeting, and the company is not a single member company

☐   A board meeting of a private company

☐   Where a meeting is held by order of the court

☐   A class meeting where all the shares are held by one member

☐   Where a meeting of five members is convened but only one turns up

8   Members wishing to remove a director at an AGM cannot insist on their resolution being included in the notice of the meeting unless they have at least:

A   5% of the paid up share capital or voting rights
B   10% of the paid up share capital or voting rights
C   15% of the paid up share capital or voting rights
D   20% of the paid up share capital or voting rights

9   Waugh Ltd, a manufacturing company, wants to make a loan of £16,000 to one of its directors for their personal use. This transaction is:

    A   Explicitly prohibited by the Companies Act 2006

    B   Explicitly prohibited by the Companies Act 2006 unless sanctioned by an ordinary resolution

    C   Explicitly prohibited by the Companies Act 2006 unless sanctioned by a special resolution

    D   Permitted under the Companies Act 2006 providing the director makes appropriate disclosure

10   Minutes of the general meeting can be inspected by:

    A   Members and creditors

    B   Members and creditors by paying a reasonable fee

    C   Members

    D   Members and customers

29 Company administration and management 2

1   A company has 5 members who are also directors. Each holds 10 shares. Normally the shares carry 1 vote each, but the articles state that on a resolution for a director's removal, the director to be removed should have 5 votes per share. On a resolution for the removal of Pamela, a director, Pamela casts 50 votes against the resolution and the other members cast 40 votes for the resolution. Has Pamela validly defeated the resolution?

    A   No. The articles are invalid insofar as they purport to confer extra votes.

    B   Yes. The proceedings and articles are valid.

    C   Yes. Whilst the articles are invalid, a special resolution is required and the necessary majority has not been obtained.

    D   No. A director is not entitled to vote on a resolution for her own removal.

2   Sophia is a director of a company which has just failed to win a valuable contract. She persuades the company to release her from her service agreement on the grounds of ill-health. Now that she is no longer a director, she feels free to attempt to obtain the contract for herself, which she successfully does. Is she accountable for this profit when the company sues her?

    A   No, since the company chose to release her from her service agreement and therefore from her obligations to it.

    B   No, since she is no longer a director and therefore no longer owes any duty.

    C   No, since the company could not have obtained the contract anyway and therefore lost nothing.

    D   Yes, she is accountable in this situation.

3   Which **three** of the following are duties of directors under the Companies Act 2006?

☐ Promote the success of the company

☐ Promote the relationship between directors and employees

☐ Declare trading losses to the stock exchange

☐ Declare an interest in an existing transaction or arrangement

☐ Exercise reasonable judgement

4   Which of the following statements concerning the duties of directors provided for in the articles are true or false?

Statement	True	False
The articles may authorise anything that might otherwise be a breach of statutory duty.		
Directors will not be liable for breaching statutory conflict of interest rules if they follow any lawful provisions for dealing with them contained in the articles.		
Articles may normally permit less onerous regulations than the Companies Act.		
Some conflicts of interest by independent directors are permissible by the articles.		

5   The quorum for a board meeting is:

A   Whatever figure the articles state or allow the directors to decide

B   Two, in all cases

C   One

D   Three, to avoid potential deadlock

6   Which of the following regarding general meetings is **incorrect?**

A   The directors have power under the articles to convene a general meeting whenever they see fit.

B   Where the members requisition the directors to call a general meeting, a signed requisition must be deposited at the registered office by the requisitioners stating the objects of the meeting.

C   Where the members requisition the directors to call a general meeting, the notice must give at least 28 days notice.

D   If there is no quorum at a general meeting requisitioned by the members, the meeting is adjourned.

7   The directors of a company allot 100,000 unissued shares to a third party, in order to thwart a takeover bid. A general meeting is called one month later, at which an ordinary resolution is passed, with the support of the votes of the newly-issued shares, ratifying the allotment. A group of minority shareholders challenge the validity of the ratification. What is the position?

   A   The ratification is valid.

   B   The ratification is invalid, but only because a special resolution is required, not an ordinary one.

   C   The ratification is invalid but only because the holder of the new shares should have been excluded from voting.

   D   The ratification is invalid, but only because the general meeting was called outside the required period after the allotment.

8   Walsall plc held its annual general meeting for approving the 20X6 accounts on 31 October 20X6. Its accounting reference date is 31 July. What is the latest date by which the next annual general meeting must be held?

   A   31 October 20X7
   B   31 December 20X7
   C   31 January 20X8
   D   30 April 20X8

9   Under which circumstance must the directors of a plc convene a general meeting?

   A   If the company makes a trading loss
   B   If the company's net assets fall to half or less of its issued share capital
   C   If the company secretary resigns
   D   If the company's net assets fall to half or less of its called-up share capital

10 John, a member of a public limited company, appoints Steve as his proxy for a forthcoming meeting. At that meeting, Steve will have the right to vote:

   A   Only on a poll
   B   Only on a poll and address the meeting
   C   Only on a show of hands
   D   On a poll, a show of hands and address the meeting

30 Company administration and management 3

1   What is the quorum for a general meeting of a public limited company?

   A   Two persons being members or proxies for members
   B   Five persons being members or proxies for members
   C   Two persons being members
   D   Five persons being members

2   If, on 1 March 20X8, the secretary of Nutley & Co Ltd called a general meeting to be held on 8 March 20X8, by sending notice in the post to all members entitled to attend and vote at the meeting, then the meeting:

A   Is void

B   Is properly notified

C   May proceed provided that a majority of members holding at least 90% of the issued shares carrying voting rights consent to short notice

D   May proceed provided all members of the company consent to short notice

3   Trends Ltd has an issued share capital of £100 in ordinary shares of £1, each carrying one vote. Larry is a shareholder in the company. He has received notice of a general meeting at which a resolution is proposed to alter the company's articles. Larry does not agree with the proposed alteration.

How many votes must Larry cast against the resolution to ensure that he defeats it at the meeting, assuming all members entitled to do so attend the meeting and vote?

A   25 votes
B   26 votes
C   50 votes
D   51 votes

4   Which of the following statements concerning directors' personal liability are true or false?

Statement	True	False
Liability may arise through lifting the veil of incorporation.		
Directors can never be liable to a company's creditors.		
A limited company may by special resolution provide that its directors have unlimited liability for its debts.		
Directors are generally liable for the acts of the other directors.		

5   An application to the court under s 994 Companies Act 2006 for a petition that a company's affairs have been conducted in an unfairly prejudicial manner can be made by:

A   The company
B   Members holding not less than 15% in number of the issued shares of the company
C   A creditor of the company
D   Any member of the company

6   Alf and Bert, who are directors and shareholders in Oakhill Ltd, have recently purchased from the company for £100,000 land which is worth £120,000. On what grounds will Cedric, a minority shareholder, be able to sue the directors in the company's name?

A   It is just and equitable to do so.
B   The directors have used their position to make a personal gain.
C   The transaction is *ultra vires* the directors.
D   The transaction is *ultra vires* the company.

7   A sale to a company of property owned by one of its directors is disclosable in its accounts. What are the consequences of non-disclosure assuming the transaction has been properly disclosed elsewhere?

   A   The sale of the property is voidable by the company.
   B   The director will hold any proceeds on constructive trust for the company.
   C   The auditors must refuse to approve the accounts and resign.
   D   The auditors must include details of the transaction in their report to members.

8   Which **three** of the following are true in relation to retirement by rotation of directors?

   ☐   Every year one third of directors should retire.
   ☐   At the first AGM all the directors should retire.
   ☐   Directors in office longest since their last election shall be retired.
   ☐   The question of who is to retire may be decided by lot.
   ☐   Retiring directors are eligible for re-election.

9   Which of the following resolutions **cannot** be made by a public company?

   A   Special resolutions
   B   Written resolutions
   C   Ordinary resolutions
   D   Any resolution requiring special notice

10   Which of the following statements about written resolutions is **correct**?

   A   Written resolutions can be used for any purpose except the removal of an auditor.
   B   Auditors have the right of objection to written resolutions.
   C   Written resolutions cannot be used if the company's articles forbid it.
   D   Written resolutions can only be used by private companies.

31 Company administration and management 4

1   Which of the following statements in relation to directors of companies limited by shares, is **incorrect**?

   A   The directors are agents of the company.
   B   At least two directors must be natural persons.
   C   An individual director who is not the managing director cannot contract on behalf of the company unless power has been delegated to them.
   D   The shareholders cannot interfere with the management of the company unless authorised by the articles of association or the law.

2   Special notice must be given of:

   A   A resolution to change a company's name
   B   A resolution to allot new shares
   C   A resolution to remove a director
   D   A resolution to appoint a director

3   What is the minimum period of notice for an AGM?

   A   7 days
   B   14 days
   C   21 days
   D   28 days

4   If a member seeks to prove that he is a 'partner' who has been excluded from participation in the management of a quasi-partnership, he must demonstrate:

   A   Mismanagement
   B   Prejudice to himself as a member
   C   Bad faith
   D   Expulsion from membership

5   Under certain circumstances a member can bring a derivative claim on behalf of the company against the directors for breach of reasonable skill, care or diligence. To whom would any damages accrue?

   A   The member
   B   The company
   C   The other members
   D   The creditors

6   Which of the following statements about the duties of directors is **correct**?

   A   The directors have a duty to ensure that no individual shareholder suffers a financial loss as a result of purchasing the company's shares.

   B   Directors owe their duties to the members.

   C   Current and past directors owe duties.

   D   Directors have a duty to distribute a dividend to ordinary shareholders each year.

7   What length of notice is required and what majority of a company's members attending and voting in person or by proxy is needed to pass an ordinary resolution at a general meeting other than an AGM?

   A   14 days notice and over 50%
   B   21 days notice and over 50%
   C   14 days notice and 75%
   D   21 days notice and 75%

8   A disqualification order against a director of a company on the ground that his conduct makes him unfit to be concerned in the management of a company may last for:

   A   A minimum of 2 years and a maximum of 5 years
   B   A minimum of 2 years and a maximum of 15 years
   C   A minimum of 5 years with no maximum
   D   A maximum of 15 years with no minimum

9   Which of the following is **not** a mitigating circumstance for the disqualification of a director?

        A   Lack of dishonesty
        B   Absence of personal gain
        C   Likelihood of repeating the offence
        D   The director was unpaid

10   The duty of directors to exercise reasonable skill and care extends to which **three** of the following?

        ☐   Managing directors
        ☐   Chairmen
        ☐   Non-executive directors
        ☐   Advisors without board positions
        ☐   All involved in the management of a company

32 Company administration and management 5

1   If a director breaches his fiduciary duty, which of the following **never** applies?

        A   The director may have to account for a secret profit if he has made one.

        B   If the director holds more than 50% of the shares he can ratify his own breach of duty at an annual
                general meeting.

        C   The director can be automatically absolved from breach of duty by the articles.

        D   The director may be liable in tort.

2   Which **three** of the following are roles of the chairman of a board meeting?

        ☐   Ensure the functions of the board are carried out.
        ☐   Provide an agenda.
        ☐   Distribute any paperwork.
        ☐   Ensure the meeting proceeds efficiently.
        ☐   Arrange a suitable location.

3   A private company has not held a meeting for eighteen months. As a minimum, what percentage of the
        voting rights do members need to requisition one?

        A   5%
        B   10%
        C   15%
        D   20%

4   Fill in the missing words.

.... directors perform specific roles in a company usually requiring daily involvement in management.

.... directors do not have any specific managerial roles except attending board meetings.

.... directors are appointed to fulfil the main management function.

.... directors are those who are not formally appointed but are with whom the board is accustomed to act in accordance

Shadow	Executive
Non-executive	Managing

5   If a meeting becomes inquorate during its proceedings:

A   The meeting may continue so long as a quorum was present at its start.
B   The meeting as a whole is a nullity.
C   The chairman may choose to adjourn at his discretion.
D   The chairman must automatically adjourn.

6   Small Ltd was incorporated on 1 August 20X6. What is the latest date on which it must hold its first annual general meeting?

A   1 August 20X7
B   1 November 20X7
C   31 December 20X7
D   Never

7   Which of the following is eligible to act as a company's auditor?

A   A spouse of an employee of the company
B   An officer of the company
C   A shareholder of the company
D   A spouse of an employee of a subsidiary of the company

8   Andrew, a director of Beth Ltd, wishes to sell his flat to the company for £70,000. What should he do?

A   Nothing; the sale is not allowed.
B   Disclose it to the shareholders only
C   Disclose it to the shareholders and all directors
D   Proceed with the sale; approval is not required for private companies

9   Omega Limited has three directors, Alpha, Beta and Gamma. Alpha works for the company full-time. Beta and Gamma (who is an experienced accountant) are non-executive directors. At Alpha's request, Beta and Gamma sign blank cheques, which Alpha then uses to make loans on behalf of Omega Limited, which are then lost. Which of the directors will be liable to the company?

   A   All three of them as in their capacity as directors they have a duty of care.

   B   Alpha only, as he is the only full-time director, the other two being non-executive.

   C   Alpha and Gamma, as the latter is an accountant and should know that signing blank cheques is negligent.

   D   None of them, as they have acted diligently and shown a reasonable degree of skill.

10   Which of the following is **not** a right of an auditor?

   A   Attendance at board meetings
   B   To receive copies of written resolutions
   C   Access to the books and accounts of the company at all times
   D   To speak at general meetings on matters concerning them as auditors

33 Corporate finance 1

1   HIJ Ltd has borrowed money from K Bank plc and has provided security by executing a fixed charge debenture in favour of the bank. A fixed charge is:

   A   A charge over specific company property which prevents the company from dealing freely with the property in the ordinary course of business.

   B   A charge over a class of company assets which enables the company to deal freely with the assets in the ordinary course of business.

   C   A charge over specific company property which enables the company to deal freely with the assets in the ordinary course of business.

   D   A charge over company land enabling the company to deal freely with the land in the ordinary course of business.

2   Companies limited by shares are subject to the 'maintenance of capital' rule. Which of the following statements regarding the rule is **incorrect**?

   A   A company cannot simply return share capital to its shareholders.

   B   Share capital must be set aside and used to pay creditors in the event of the company becoming insolvent.

   C   Share capital should be used to further a company's lawful objectives.

   D   Share capital may be returned to the shareholders following an approved reduction of capital scheme.

3   If a company issues new ordinary shares for cash, the general rule is that:

A   The shares must be offered to the existing members rateably in the case of a public but not a private company.

B   The shares must be offered to the existing members rateably in the case of a private but not a public company.

C   The shares must be offered to the existing members rateably whether the company is public or private.

D   The shares need not be issued to the existing members rateably.

4   If the net assets of a public company are half or less of the amount of its called up share capital, the directors must call a general meeting. Within what period from their becoming aware of the need to do so must they issue a notice convening the meeting?

A   7 days
B   21 days
C   28 days
D   3 months

5   Which **three** things may be required to enable a private company to reduce capital?

☐   Pass an ordinary resolution with the usual notice
☐   Pass a special resolution with the usual notice
☐   Obtain permission of the court
☐   Produce a solvency statement
☐   Amend the statement of Capital and Initial Shareholdings

6   In relation to company charges, which of the following is **correct**?

A   A private company cannot create fixed charges.
B   A public company cannot create floating charges.
C   Both private and public companies may create fixed and floating charges.
D   All business organisations can create fixed and floating charges.

7   Which of the following statements concerning the variation of class rights are true or false?

Examples of variation of class rights include:

Statement	True	False
Returning capital to the holders of preference shares		
Issuing a new class of preference share with priority over an existing class of ordinary share		
Reduction of voting rights attached to a class of share		
Issuing shares of a particular class to allottees who are not already members of that class		

8   Authority given to directors to allot shares can be granted by:

    A   A provision in the articles only

    B   A special resolution only

    C   A special resolution or a provision in the articles only

    D   An ordinary resolution, a special resolution or provision in the articles

9   Which of the following may give financial assistance to another company for the purchase of its own shares?

    A   A private company only

    B   A public company only

    C   Both private and public companies

    D   Public companies only, but assistance can only be given to a private subsidiary

10   Which of the following is an allowable use of the share premium account?

    A   To pay issue costs in respect of a new share issue

    B   To pay capital costs on forming a company

    C   To pay dividends

    D   To repurchase debentures

34 Corporate finance 2

1   A private company has an issued share capital (fully paid) of £90,000, £10,000 on its share premium account and a negative balance of £5,000 on its revaluation reserve. Its net assets are £112,500. What is the maximum amount that it can distribute as dividend?

    A   £12,500

    B   £17,500

    C   £22,500

    D   It cannot pay a dividend

2   A floating charge is created on 1 March 20X2 and crystallises on 1 October 20X2. A fixed charge over the same property is created on 1 September 20X2. Assuming both are registered within the prescribed time limits, which ranks first?

    A   The fixed charge.

    B   The floating charge.

    C   On crystallisation of the floating charge to a fixed charge, both rank *pari passu* (as fixed charges).

    D   The floating charge becomes a fixed charge on crystallisation, and at that point ranks before the original fixed charge.

3   Which of the following statements is **correct**?

   A   A public company can issue shares at a discount.

   B   A public company's shares can never be partly paid up.

   C   A public company can issue shares in return for an undertaking to do work or perform services.

   D   A public company must obtain an independent valuation for non-cash consideration for its shares from its auditor.

4   It appears that Unsteady Ltd is about to go into liquidation owing its creditors considerable sums of money. Are the following statements true or false?

Statement	True	False
The directors will always be liable to recompense the company's creditors.		
The directors may be liable to recompense the company's creditors.		
The members will always be liable to recompense the company's creditors.		
The members will never be liable to recompense the company's creditors.		

5   A company creates a charge in June in favour of its bank. The necessary documents are executed, but left undated and not registered by the bank's solicitor. In November he realises his mistake, writes a November date on the documents and registers them within the specified period from that date. A certificate of registration is issued. In December the company goes into voluntary liquidation. The liquidator challenges the validity of the charge on the grounds that it was not registered within the specified time after its creation. Is the charge valid and enforceable?

   A   No. The charge was registered out of time.
   B   No. The charge was registered fraudulently and the solicitor can be sued.
   C   Yes. The certificate is valid and conclusive.
   D   Yes, but only if the court orders rectification of the certificate.

6   Under the Companies Act a shareholder has a statutory right of pre-emption:

   A   On the allotment of equity shares for cash by the company
   B   On any allotment of shares by the company
   C   On a transfer of shares by another member of the same company
   D   On the transmission of shares on the death of another member of the same company

7   James Ltd wishes to reduce its issued share capital. Which **three** of these requirements must the company meet in order to do so?

☐   Power to do so must be included in the Articles

☐   The company must pass a special resolution

☐   The company must obtain the confirmation of the court or issue a statement of solvency to proceed with the scheme

☐   The company must obtain written authorisation by its auditor

☐   The Registrar must be informed

8   Which of the following is a right of a secured debenture holder?

A   To take possession of the asset if the charge is a fixed charge.
B   To appoint a receiver of the asset even if an administration order is in force.
C   To place the company into administration if the charge is a fixed charge.
D   To receive annual dividends if the charge is a floating charge.

9   The directors of Pen Ltd are proposing a purchase by the company of its own shares out of capital. They have made a statutory declaration and called a general meeting of members. What kind of resolution is required to approve this proposal?

A   Ordinary resolution
B   Ordinary resolution with special notice
C   Special resolution with special notice
D   Special resolution

10   Where the net assets of a public company are half or less of its called-up share capital the directors have a statutory duty to convene a general meeting of the company. The purpose of this meeting is to

A   Pass a special resolution to initiate a members' voluntary winding-up
B   Pass an ordinary resolution to initiate a creditors' voluntary winding-up
C   Pass a special resolution for the reduction of issued capital
D   Consider the steps, if any, that should be taken to deal with the situation

35 Corporate finance 3

1   HIJ Ltd has borrowed money from K Bank plc and has provided security by executing a floating charge debenture in favour of the bank. A floating charge is:

A   A charge over specific company property which prevents the company from dealing freely with the property in the ordinary course of business.
B   A charge over a class of company assets which enables the company to deal freely with the assets in the ordinary course of business.
C   A charge over specific company property which enables the company to deal freely with the assets in the ordinary course of business.
D   A charge over company land enabling the company to deal freely with the land in the ordinary course of business.

2   Which of the following is the correct period within which company charges must be registered with the Registrar of companies?

    A   7 days following the issue of the charge
    B   14 days following the issue of the charge
    C   21 days following the issue of the charge
    D   28 days following the issue of the charge

3   Which **three** of the following are exceptions to the general rule that a company may not purchase its own shares?

☐ Redemption of redeemable shares

☐ Purchase of shares under the reduction of capital procedures

☐ Purchase of shares in compliance with a court order

☐ Purchase of own shares if a shareholder has made a bid for 90% of the issue share capital

☐ Purchase of own shares by a quoted company

4   Which of the following statements regarding the relationship between ordinary shares and debentures is **incorrect**?

    A   Debentures do not normally confer voting rights, whilst ordinary shares do.

    B   The company has a duty to pay interest on debentures, and to pay dividends on ordinary shares.

    C   Interest paid on debentures is deducted from pre-tax profits, share dividends are paid from net profits.

    D   A debentureholder takes priority over a member in liquidation.

5   Under which circumstance can unlawful dividends be reclaimed?

    A   By members when directors are paid dividends out of capital
    B   By the company from members who knew them to be unlawful
    C   By creditors when directors paid dividends from an undistributable reserve
    D   By members of one class when unlawful dividends are paid out to members of another class.

6   A private company has amended its articles to disapply the statutory right of pre-emption under s 570. The resolution was combined with a grant of authority to the directors to allot shares. What is the maximum permitted duration of the resolution?

    A   There is no limit to the duration of the resolution
    B   3 months
    C   1 year
    D   5 years

7   After a purchase of its own shares by either a market or off-market method, the company must make a return to the Registrar under s 701 within:

    A   7 days
    B   21 days
    C   28 days
    D   3 months

8   Which of the following is **not** an undistributable reserve?

    A   Share premium account
    B   Capital redemption reserve
    C   A surplus of accumulated unrealised profits over accumulated unrealised losses
    D   Contingency reserve

9   If there has been a variation of class rights, a minority of holders of shares of the class (who have not consented or voted in favour of the variation) may apply to the court to have the variation cancelled. The objectors must:

    A   Hold not less than 15% of the issued shares of that class and apply to the court within 28 days of the giving of consent by the class.

    B   Hold not less than 10% of the issued shares of that class and apply to the court within 28 days of the giving of consent by the class.

    C   Hold not less than 15% of the issued shares of that class and apply to the court within 21 days of the giving of consent by the class.

    D   Hold not less than 10% of the issued shares of that class and apply to the court within 2 calendar months of the giving of consent by the class.

10   A register of debentureholders is required:

    A   By law in all cases
    B   By law in some cases
    C   By a contractual term (if any) of the debenture
    D   By order of the court

36 Corporate finance 4

1   A company wishes to issue debentures and shares at a discount to their nominal value. Are the issues valid?

    A   Debentures no, shares yes
    B   Debentures yes, shares no
    C   Debentures no, shares no
    D   Debentures yes, shares yes

2   A company has a nominal capital of £600,000 divided into 600,000 shares of £1 each, of which £400,000 is issued and only £100,000 is paid up. What is the amount of the uncalled capital that may be called up at 14 days' notice?

A   £200,000
B   £300,000
C   £400,000
D   £500,000

3   If a company is wound up insolvent what is the effect of non-registration of a floating charge under the Companies Act?

A   The debt is void against the liquidator and the chargee receives nothing.
B   The charge is voidable by the liquidator if the company was insolvent when the charge was created.
C   The charge is void against the liquidator and the chargee proceeds as an ordinary creditor.
D   The charge is void against subsequent secured creditors and the chargee loses priority accordingly.

4   A floating charge is created by a company nine months before it goes into liquidation. The charge is in favour of a bank to secure an existing debt. The charge is:

A   Valid as a fixed charge
B   Valid as a floating charge
C   Automatically invalid
D   Voidable by the liquidator as a fraudulent preference

5   Where a listed plc legitimately purchases 10% of its own shares out of profit, it may hold them as:

A   Deferred shares
B   Redeemable shares
C   Treasury shares
D   Preference shares

6   Profits available for distribution in a private company may be defined as:

A   Accumulated realised profits less accumulated realised losses
B   Accumulated realised profits less losses for the current year
C   Accumulated realised profits
D   Accumulated realised profits less accumulated realised and unrealised losses

7   What are the consequences for the shareholders of a public company if the directors make a distribution in excess of the amount permitted by the Companies Act?

A   The total distribution is repayable to the company by all the shareholders.

B   The excess amount over that permitted is repayable by all shareholders.

C   The excess over the permitted amount is repayable by shareholders who knew or had reasonable grounds to believe that the distribution was in contravention of the Act.

D   The amount repayable is the total amount that was paid to shareholders who knew, or had reasonable grounds to believe, the distribution to be in contravention of the Act.

8   Which of the following is **not** a constitutional source of rights attaching to a particular class of share?

A   The articles of association
B   A special resolution by the company in general meeting
C   Prospectus of a new share issue
D   A shareholders' agreement

9   Which of the following schemes involves a reduction of capital, requiring the confirmation of the court?

A   A repayment of preference shares and the re-dating of £100,000 debentures from 20X2 to 20X9.

B   A reconstruction involving the transfer of assets from one company to another with a members' voluntary winding up of the old company.

C   The reduction in nominal value of shares from 100 pence to 80 pence by the cancellation of a call not yet made.

D   The provision of financial assistance by way of loan for the purchase of shares in the company.

10   The directors of Cob Ltd are proposing a purchase by the company of its own shares out of capital. They have made a statutory declaration and called a general meeting of members to approve their proposal.

The statutory declaration made by the directors must contain a statement that in their opinion the company will be able to carry on business as a going concern and will be able to pay its debts as they fall due in the next:

A   Six months
B   Year
C   Eighteen months
D   Two years

37 Ethics and business 1

1   Which statement describes the principle of objectivity?

A   By following this principle, an accountant minimises the risk of passing on incorrect information.
B   Following this principle requires an accountant to keep their mind free from bias.
C   Following this principle requires an accountant to stay technically up to date.
D   Following this principle requires scepticism and close attention to detail when reviewing information.

2   Under which circumstance might an accountant have to disclose information given to them in confidence?

A   When requested by a regulator
B   When requested by a lawyer
C   When requested by a fellow employee or client
D   When requested by an employer

3 An accountant who refuses to take on work as they do not have any experience in that area can be said to be arguing what?

A   Integrity
B   Professional behaviour
C   Objectivity
D   Professional competence

4 Which **three** of the following allow accountants to demonstrate the professional quality of scepticism?

☐	By keeping their mind free from distractions.
☐	By seeking supporting evidence before accepting information is accurate.
☐	By investigating why information was given to them.
☐	By reviewing the work of a junior before accepting it as correct.
☐	By being straightforward and honest at all times.

5 How can accountants demonstrate accountability?

A   By questioning work given to them.
B   By taking responsibility for a mistake.
C   By ensuring their work is free from error.
D   By replying to an email on behalf of a colleague.

6 Which of the following is an example of an accountant's social responsibility?

A   To increase the profitability of the business they work for.
B   To ensure the maximum corporation tax is paid by their employer.
C   To use recycling facilities if provided by their employer.
D   To provide accurate financial information to shareholders.

7 Which **three** of the following are virtues explicitly contained in the CIMA Code of practice?

☐	Financial responsibility
☐	Respect
☐	Social responsibility
☐	Courtesy
☐	Confidence

8 Which of the following statements best describes the relationship between the Code of Ethics of CIMA and IFAC?

A   CIMA's framework is generally the same as IFAC's with some amendments to ensure it meets other regulatory requirements.

B   IFAC provides the detailed rules that CIMA must include in its code.

C   CIMA has picked the most important elements of the IFAC code for inclusion into its own.

D   IFAC's code is based on international standards whereas CIMA's is specific to the UK.

9   The following statements all concern the Seven Principles of Public Life.

Fill in the missing words.

The principle of .... means that individuals should act solely in the public interest and not for personal gain.

To meet the principle of .... individuals should declare private interests that relate to their public ones.

By ensuring information regarding the reasons for their decisions are freely available means that individuals meet the principle of ....

.... involves the promotion and respect of the six other principles.

Leadership	Openness
Selflessness	Honesty

10   Which of the following statements is **correct**?

A   The Professional Oversight Board contains two sub-bodies, the Financial Reporting Council and the Auditing Practices Board.

B   The Auditing Practices Board issues ethical standards for auditors.

C   The Financial Reporting Council is mainly concerned with the ethics of the accountancy profession.

D   The Professional Oversight Board is mainly concerned with the conduct and discipline of accountants.

38 Ethics and business 2

1   Which **three** of the following explain why the principle of integrity is important?

☐ To prevent passing on misinformation.
☐ To prevent bias affecting an accountant's work.
☐ To enhance the credibility of an accountant's work.
☐ To protect the security of information.
☐ To ensure straightforward and honest dealings.

2   Which of the following statements best describes corporate responsibility?

A   The company must appear ethically in all its marketing materials.

B   The company must put the needs of the community, its shareholders and employees at the heart of all its decisions.

C   The company develops policies on issues such as how to support the local community and charities to ensure it plays a positive role in its local area.

D   The company must develop relationships with its stakeholders so it can learn from them and meet their needs in a more efficient and environmentally friendly way.

3   Along with courtesy and timeliness, what are the other three personal qualities expected of accountants?

A   Respect, reliability, responsibility
B   Realism, reliability, regulation
C   Reliability, reflection, responsibility
D   Responsibility, reliability, realism

4   Why has IFAC issued a code of ethics for accountants worldwide?

A   It was requested to do so by the World Bank.
B   Worldwide corporate scandals have eroded all confidence in accountants.
C   To enhance the quality and standards of services provided by accountants.
D   International law has required a worldwide code of ethics.

5   Business wisdom suggests there are three elements to creating an effective ethical programme. Which of the following is **not** one of these elements?

A   Buy-in
B   Enforcement
C   Training
D   Active leadership

6   Fill in the missing words

An accountant's quality of .... will help safeguard confidential information as they do not take undue risks that could result in the information being made public.

Another feature of this quality is they ensure their work is complete and meets .... standards.

The quality of .... means accountants should own up to mistakes and face the consequences. This means it is important that they demonstrate .... when reviewing information and making decisions.

Professional	Scepticism
Accountability	Responsibility

7   Which one of the following is **incorrect**? Accountants must be up to date with technical and professional developments because

A   CIMA's code of ethics requires this.
B   The Seven Principles of Public Life require this.
C   They have a professional duty to do this.
D   Clients have a right to competent service.

8   Which of the following statements concerning codes of ethics is **incorrect**?

A   IFAC's code is based on compliance principles.

B   The code of ethics of a business may take either a compliance or ethics based approach.

C   CIMA's code is based on an ethical framework.

D   Many codes of ethics require individuals to respect the spirit of the law rather than the letter of the law.

9   CIMA's code of ethics has several purposes. Which of the following is most likely to be a legitimate purpose?

A   It provides members with all of their legal obligations in one document.
B   It is evidence that all CIMA members meet IFAC's requirements for ethical behaviour.
C   It is a requirement of its status as a chartered organisation.
D   It can be used to judge the behaviour of members under CIMA's disciplinary procedures.

10   Which of the Seven Principles of Public Life requires individuals to avoid actions that may place them under financial or other obligations whereby the person holding their obligations could influence their public duties?

A   Objectivity
B   Openness
C   Integrity
D   Selflessness

39 Ethics and business 3

1   There are many reasons why CIMA members should follow CIMA's ethical code. Which of the following is **incorrect**?

A   All CIMA members must follow CIMA's code as a condition of their membership.
B   All CIMA members are obliged to follow IFAC's code as CIMA is a member of IFAC.
C   CIMA members are legally bound by CIMA's code.
D   CIMA's code encourages best practice and is in the public interest.

2   How can an accountant demonstrate independence?

A   By double-checking their work.
B   By avoiding situations that might cause an observer to doubt their objectivity.
C   By questioning the work of others.
D   By considering the needs of their colleagues at work.

3   One of the following actions by a CIMA member would not help them act either in the public interest or in a socially responsible manner. Which action is this?

A   Ensuring they act in accordance with CIMA's ethical code.
B   Setting their personal and career goals.
C   Attending relevant training programmes.
D   Demonstrating responsibility.

4   Several judgements and decisions made by an accountant have been found to be ill judged. The accountant takes full responsibility for this. Which professional quality are they demonstrating?

   A   Social responsibility
   B   Scepticism
   C   Independence
   D   Accountability

5   Ethical codes such as those developed by IFAC and CIMA should:

   A   Enhance the standards of their members
   B   Eliminate unethical behaviour by members
   C   Indicate the highest level of behaviour expected of members
   D   Always consist of fundamental principles

6   Compliance-based and ethics-based approaches to codes of ethics can be described using different phrases. Indicate which phrase is appropriate to which approach.

Phrase	Compliance-based	Ethics-based
Law based		
Detection		
Principles based		
Discretionary		

7   Which part of IFAC's ethical code contains the main guidance for professional accountants in business?

   A   Part A
   B   Part B
   C   Part C
   D   Part D

8   Which **three** of the following are included within CIMA's fundamental principles?

   ☐   Professional behaviour
   ☐   Leadership
   ☐   Confidentiality
   ☐   Professional competence
   ☐   Openness

9   How does a framework-based approach to developing an ethical code differ from a rules-based approach?

   A   It sets out specific guidance for each specific ethical dilemma.
   B   It expects members to adhere to the letter of the law.
   C   It expects members to embody certain principles.
   D   The governing body anticipates all potential ethical problems.

10   Which of the following is **not** a stage in CIMA's Professional Development Cycle?

    A   Act
    B   Design
    C   Reflect
    D   Review

40 Ethical conflict 1

1   It has been brought to your attention that a colleague in your accounts department has been continually submitting inflated expenses claims. Which of CIMA's fundamental principles have they breached?

    A   Objectivity
    B   Integrity
    C   Professional behaviour
    D   Confidentiality

2   You are the finance director of a large multinational company which has recently expanded its operations. The expansion was funded by loans supplied by Bramble Bank. The finance director of Bramble Bank has offered you a free holiday at his luxury villa and use of his private jet. If you accept which of CIMA's fundamental principles will you break?

    A   Objectivity
    B   Integrity
    C   Professional behaviour
    D   Confidentiality

3   You are aware that a colleague regularly takes important reports home to check, but does so after drinking a bottle of wine. Are they in breach of any of CIMA's fundamental principles, if so which one?

    A   There is no breach of fundamental principles.
    B   Professional competence and due care.
    C   Objectivity
    D   Integrity

4   You are the management accountant of a large chain of health clubs. Your father has decided to set up his own rival chain and has asked you to become finance director. However, as a condition he has asked you to provide him with the database of members' details from your current employer. If you go ahead, which of CIMA's fundamental principles will you break?

    A   Professional competence and due care
    B   Integrity
    C   Objectivity
    D   Confidentiality

5   Your manager has set out a new policy that you should follow when preparing the management accounts. From now on you are to use estimates for trade receivables and payables. Does this conflict with any of CIMA's fundamental principles, if so which one?

    A   No, it does not conflict with any of CIMA's principles

    B   Integrity

    C   Objectivity

    D   Professional competence and due care

6   When a CIMA member faces an ethical conflict, who should they look to first to resolve it?

    A   CIMA

    B   The board of directors

    C   Themselves

    D   Relevant outside professional advisors

7   Fill in the missing words.

    Ethical dilemmas often occur as a result of tension between four sets of values. .... values are represented by the law, ...…... values are held by the organisation that an individual is a member of, ...…... values are those held by the individual and .... values are those held by the organisation which employs the individual.

Personal	Professional
Corporate	Societal

8   Which of the following best describes CIMA's fundamental principle of professional competence?

    A   Owning up when you think that you are not suitably experienced to perform a role.

    B   Refusing to take on work where there is a conflict of interest.

    C   Accepting responsibility when things go wrong.

    D   Ensuring private information remains private.

9   Which **three** of the following are potential consequences to the accounting profession if members are allowed to behave unethically?

    ☐   Professional bodies may lose their 'chartered' status.

    ☐   Increased regulation of the profession by external organisations.

    ☐   Increased employability of accountants.

    ☐   Improved reputation of the profession.

    ☐   Reduced public trust in the profession.

10   What should a CIMA member do if the only option available to resolve an ethical issue with their employer involves breach of confidentiality?

    A   Proceed with the solution

    B   Take legal advice before proceeding

    C   Do not proceed with the resolution

    D   Take advice from friends and family

41 Ethical conflict 2

1   Where a professional duty conflicts with the law, which should be followed?

    A   The professional duty
    B   The professional duty if it agrees with the individual's personal ethics
    C   The law
    D   The law, only it if agrees with the individual's personal ethics

2   Which of the following statements are true or false?

Statement	True	False
Unethical behaviour will always be punished with a criminal conviction		
CIMA students are expected to demonstrate the same level of professional standards as full members.		
A conflict of interest is evidence of wrongdoing.		
Societal values are encompassed in the law.		

3   Which of the following examples of unethical behaviour could an accountant face criminal prosecution for if committed?

    A   Sending an abusive email
    B   Supplying confidential information about a public listed company to a stock broker
    C   Supplying management accounts to directors that are inaccurate
    D   Allowing personal problems to interfere with the production of management accounts

4   A CIMA member has encountered a fraud but it would breach confidentiality if it were to be disclosed. What should the member do?

    A   Disclose the fraud without delay
    B   Seek legal advice or consult CIMA
    C   Respect the confidence and avoid disclosure
    D   Take steps to resolve the fraud personally.

5   A colleague has provided a report to senior management that contains misleading information. Which of CIMA's fundamental principles have they broken?

    A   Integrity
    B   Confidentiality
    C   Professional competence and due care
    D   Objectivity

6   Which **three** of the following situations may create a conflict of interest?

☐   Working part-time for two rival businesses.

☐   Owning shares in a company that competes with your employer.

☐   Being employed by a close relative.

☐   Being offered a valuable gift by a friend who is also a business contact.

☐   Receiving a performance bonus from your manager.

7   Which of the following is not a benefit of ethical accountants to society?

A   Credible, accurate and reliable financial statements for investors.

B   Government collecting the correct amount of corporation tax (where accountants are used to calculate the charge).

C   Assistance to the authorities for the detection and prevention of fraud.

D   Ensuring companies are profitable.

8   Which **three** matters should CIMA members record whilst attempting to resolve an ethical issue?

☐   Meetings that take place.

☐   Decisions that are taken.

☐   Informal discussions and phone calls.

☐   Their day-to-day feelings.

☐   Advice from their families.

9   Which of the following is the least suitable to consult with when dealing with a major ethical dilemma?

A   CIMA
B   The Audit Committee of your organisation
C   Your line manager
D   A close colleague

10   You have just encountered a threat to your professional standards, what should your response be?

A   Proceed with the activity after taking legal advice.
B   Evaluate the threat and proceed with the activity but cautiously.
C   Avoid the activity
D   Consult CIMA

42 Ethical conflict 3

1   Which **three** of the following situations would justify disclosure of confidential information?

☐   To reply to a solicitor who is representing a past employee who is suing your employer.

☐   To enable the accurate preparation of a report for a departmental manager.

☐   When the person the information concerns has given you permission.

☐   To defend yourself in a claim for misconduct.

☐   When you are obliged legally.

2   Which of the following statements is **incorrect**?

A   An accountant should leave their job if their employer does not provide sufficient ethical safeguards.

B   An accountant is always absolved from liability if they did not have explicit knowledge of an ethical problem.

C   Ethical dilemmas may be both financial and non-financial.

D   CIMA students are expected to demonstrate the same level of professional standards as full members.

3   Which of the following statements about ethical dilemmas is **correct**?

A   Ethical dilemmas involve unclear choices about what is right and wrong.

B   Ethical dilemmas involve clear choices about what is right and wrong.

C   To resolve an ethical dilemma, an accountant should never trust their instincts.

D   To resolve an ethical dilemma, an accountant should never seek advice.

4   An accountant is employed by a manufacturing company, but has permission to take on private work in their spare time producing management accounts for their own clients.

Which **three** of the following situations may create a conflict of interest?

☐   Taking on work from a company that is in direct competition with their employer

☐   When the income from one private client exceeds the salary received from their main employer

☐   A private client asks the accountant to work for them full-time

☐   Having to turn down private work as they do not have sufficient spare time to do the work

☐   When the accountant needs to leave their employer's office to deal with an emergency with a private client.

5   Which of the following fundamental principles would be most at risk when an accountant is rushing to meet a deadline?

A   Professional competence

B   Integrity

C   Objectivity

D   Confidentiality

6   When taking on a new type of work for the first time, you are at greater risk of breaching which of CIMA's fundamental principles?

        A   Integrity
        B   Objectivity
        C   Professional behaviour
        D   Professional competence and due care

7   When deciding on whether a solution to an ethical dilemma is appropriate, which of the following questions is irrelevant?

        A   Do I feel comfortable about others knowing about my decision?
        B   Have I considered all parties who may be affected by my decision?
        C   Would a reasonable third party consider my decision fair?
        D   Is this the most appropriate decision considering my career aspirations?

8   Fill in the missing words.

        When considering a course of action to resolve an ethical issue, an accountant should consider the
        .... facts, CIMA's fundamental .... the ....
        issues and any .... procedures available to them.

Principles	Ethical
Internal	Relevant

9   Which of the following circumstances is most likely to cause an accountant to breach the fundamental principle of objectivity?

        A   Being asked to act contrary to professional standards
        B   Being offered gifts or hospitality
        C   Being asked to act beyond their skills and experience
        D   Being asked to turn a blind eye to fraud.

10   An accountant has been asked by their manager to amend a set of accounts contrary to established accounting standards. Which sets of values are conflicting?

        A   Corporate and professional
        B   Professional and personal
        C   Personal and corporate
        D   Professional and societal

43 Corporate governance 1

1   In October 2004 the European Union Corporate Governance Forum was established. How many members does it have?

        A   9
        B   12
        C   15
        D   18

2   In the USA, a major corporate scandal involved Enron. The company withheld certain information so that confidence in it was generated. What type of information was withheld?

        A   Loan commitments.
        B   Directors' remuneration packages
        C   Trading losses
        D   Financial restructuring

3   Which **three** of the following are reasons for the need to develop corporate governance rules?

      ☐   Active management by Fund Managers
      ☐   Stock market crashes in the 1990's
      ☐   Loss of confidence in financial statements and company management
      ☐   A number of high profile scandals and corporate collapses
      ☐   A poor standard of company legislation.

4   Which of the following statements concerning corporate governance are true or false?

Corporate governance is concerned with

Statement	True	False
Business efficacy		
Fiduciary duties of directors		
Accountability		
Profitability		

5   Performance bonuses for directors should only adversely affect a company if:

        A   The bonuses are paid in cash
        B   The bonuses are in the form of shares
        C   Directors make short-term decisions to achieve them
        D   Directors have to improve a company's share price to achieve them

6   How has the Combined Code affected executive directors' duty of skill and care?

        A   No change
        B   Increased the level of duty
        C   Reduced the level of duty
        D   Made the level of duty statutory

7   Which of the following is **not** an interest stakeholder of a company?

        A   Employees
        B   The media
        C   Competitors
        D   Regulators

8   German companies are based on a two-tier board structure. What are the names of the two boards?

     A   Policy, Supervisory
     B   Supervisory, Management
     C   Functional, Policy
     D   Executive, Management

9   What structure does the Combined Code recommend for remuneration committees when reviewing executive directors' remuneration packages?

     A   Mainly executive directors
     B   Mainly non-executive directors
     C   Exclusively executive directors
     D   There should be at least three non-executive directors

10   Match the name of the committee/report with the corporate governance issue it reported on.

     (a)   Turnbull Committee
     (b)   Smith Report
     (c)   Higgs Report

     (i)   Non-executive directors
     (ii)   Internal controls and risk management
     (iii) Audit committees

44 Corporate governance 2

1   Which statement describes corporate governance?

     A   The system by which companies are directed and controlled.
     B   The duties placed on the board of directors by the stock exchange.
     C   Regulations by which shareholders can hold directors to account for their actions.
     D   The concept that directors must act in a socially responsible manner.

2   Which board, created by the Sarbanes-Oxley Act, is responsible for policing auditors?

     A   The Public Oversight Board for Auditors
     B   The Public Company Accounting Oversight Board
     C   The Public Company Auditors Oversight Board
     D   The Accounting and Auditing Oversight Board

3   Executive directors should not have service contracts longer than three years in duration according to which of the following committee reports?

     A   Higgs
     B   Hampel
     C   Turnbull
     D   Cadbury

4 The European Commission recognised that a common approach to corporate governance was needed within the European Union, so it took which of the following actions?

 A It issued regulations
 B It issued directives
 C It created a European Code of Corporate Governance
 D It created the European Committee for Corporate Governance

5 According to *Tricker (1996)* three of the following are board structures found in the UK. Which one is **not** one of them?

 A All non-executive
 B All executive
 C Majority non-executive
 D Majority executive

6 A board of directors should monitor various aspects of the business. Which **three** of the following are examples of what it should monitor?

 ☐ The qualifications of employees

 ☐ The risk and control systems

 ☐ The communication of its strategies through the organisation

 ☐ The human capital within the business

 ☐ The bank account balance

7 Which of the following statements concerning the UK's Combined Code are true or false?

Statement	True	False
Listed companies must state in their accounts that they complied or did not comply with the Combined Code.		
Non-compliance with the Code creates a civil liability that the directors may be sued for.		
Non-compliance with the Code may result in the directors being liable for wrongful trading.		
Directors of non-compliant companies may be disqualified from acting as a director for up to five years.		

8 German boards are often based on a two-tier arrangement containing a supervisory and a management board. Which of the following is not a role of the management board?

 A Preparing resolutions for meetings
 B Providing financial statements for meetings
 C Ensuring the business meets its regulatory obligations
 D Safeguarding stakeholder interests

9   How often does the Combined Code recommend directors review the internal controls of their company?

     A   Every year
     B   Every 2 years
     C   Every 3 years
     D   As often as the directors feel necessary

10   Name the main source of corporate governance rules in the UK.

     A   The Companies Act
     B   Sarbanes-Oxley Act
     C   The Combined Code
     D   The Cadbury Report

45 Corporate governance 3

1   Which **three** of the following are examples of corporate governance?

- [ ] Internal controls to protect a company's assets
- [ ] The board of directors providing employees with a mission statement
- [ ] Stock exchange rules that dictate when shareholders may buy and sell shares
- [ ] An employee performance related pay scheme
- [ ] CIMA's Fundamental Principles

2   Which **three** of the following are financial stakeholders in a business?

- [ ] Shareholders
- [ ] Regulators
- [ ] Suppliers
- [ ] Competitors
- [ ] The Government

3   Boards in many countries operate a unitary structure. Which of the following contains two countries that mainly use such an arrangement?

     A   UK and USA
     B   UK and Germany
     C   USA and Germany
     D   France and Germany

4   Which of the following is an example of socially responsible behaviour by a business?

     A   Ensuring the chairman and chief executive roles are not performed by the same person
     B   Ensuring employees receive health and safety training
     C   Ensuring employees have access to recycling facilities
     D   Ensuring staff are hired on the basis of ability regardless of age, sex, religion or any disabilities

5 Corporate governance rules are required because:

A Shareholders want to be able to sue directors.
B Stock markets do not trust financial statements.
C Management need encouragement to act in the best interests of all stakeholders.
D Companies do not always behave ethically.

6 Shareholder activism means:

A The level of shareholder activity within the stock market generally.
B The level of involvement shareholders have in the running of a company.
C The likelihood of shareholders bringing unethical directors to account.
D The balance of power between shareholders and directors.

7 What structure does the Combined Code recommend for audit committees?

A Mainly non-executive directors.
B Mainly executive directors.
C The committee should be equally balanced between executive and non-executive directors.
D At least 3 independent non-executive directors.

8 Which of the following is an example of good corporate governance?

A Domination by a single individual
B Lack of board involvement
C Regular contact with shareholders
D Emphasis on short-term profitability

9 What requires listed companies to comply with the Combined Code?

A The Companies Act
B The London Stock Exchange
C The Higgs report
D The Financial Standards Authority

10 All companies have relationships between ethics, social responsibility, law and corporate governance. Which of the following statements is **correct**?

A Company law is drafted to be compatible with the code of ethics of most businesses.
B Ethical behaviour is obligatory, however social responsibility is optional.
C Policies of social responsibility must not clash with the values of the company.
D Many corporate governance requirements are incompatible with ethical codes.

Answers

1 English and alternative legal systems 1

1   B   The balance of probabilities (D) applies in civil cases.

2   ☐   The principle that once a court has made a ruling on a particular case, then the same
         decision will be reached in any future similar case, forms the basis of delegated legislation.

    ☑   The term 'case law' is used to describe judge-made laws stemming from courts'
         decisions.

    ☑   European Regulations become law in member nations without the member nation having
         to pass legislation.

    ☐   In the United Kingdom, legislation is introduced into Parliament by the Crown.

    ☑   Equity is a source of the law of trusts

    Principles from a court actually mean precedent not delegated legislation. Members of Parliament
    usually introduce new legislation.

3   ☑   All criminal cases, regardless of their gravity, are introduced in the Magistrates' court.

    ☐   The County Court hears civil and criminal cases.

    ☑   The Court of Appeal binds all courts below it and also normally itself.

    ☑   The House of Lords (Supreme Court for the United Kingdom) only hears civil cases if the
         point of law is in the public interest.

    ☐   The Queens Bench Division of the High Court deals with company law cases.

    The County Court only hears civil cases, the Queens Bench Divisions hears contract and tort
    cases.

4   B   The other three all do have the force of legislation.

5   C   An act prohibited by law is a crime, which is prosecuted by the state. Tort is to do with the
         infringement of individual rights and is prosecuted by individuals.

6   C   The Court of Appeal is superior to all UK courts except the House of Lords (Supreme Court for the
         United Kingdom). It is also bound by its own previous decisions. Outside the UK, it is also bound
         by the ECJ.

7   A   Option B describes the literal rule, C the mischief rule and D the contextual rule.

8   A   A High Court judge is only compelled to follow a previous decision if it is binding on him and if
         the material facts are similar. To do this he must follow the **ratio decidendi**, not the **obiter dicta**
         (hence (ii) is incorrect). He is only bound by it if it was made by a court of higher status than the
         High Court – (iv) is incorrect because it includes the decisions of a Crown Court, and also of a
         High Court which in fact are not always binding on the future decisions of a High Court.

9   B   Courts can declare the legislation void if the minister exceeded his powers. They can also strike
         out any piece of delegated legislation because it conflicts with the European Convention on
         Human Rights, not because it is contrary to public policy (so A is wrong).

10 C   Co-decision is used by the Parliament to agree proposals with the Council.

2 English and alternative legal systems 2

1   D   Employment issues are dealt with exclusively in tribunals.

2   D   Criminal law is concerned with punishment. Civil law aims to compensate, recover property or enforce legal obligations.

3   D   In Option A, not all precedents are binding (for example, if the material facts differ or the previous court had a lower status). In Option B, the UK Parliament is the main original source of legislation. In Option C, the European Court of Human Rights is the final court of appeal for human rights cases, so it does have some authority.

4   A   This literally means 'the reason for deciding'.

5   B   Option C is wrong because there is a rigid status structure for courts following judicial precedent. Option D is wrong because decisions are only binding on the recipient.

6   B   Since the *Caparo* case, it is clear that the auditor's duty of care not to act negligently is owed to the company only.

7   European Commission, European Parliament, European Council, European Court of Justice.

8

☑	There must be a sufficient relationship of proximity between defendant and claimant.
☑	It must be reasonable that the defendant should foresee that damage might arise from his carelessness.
☐	The claimant must have acted in good faith.
☑	It must be just and reasonable for the law to impose liability.
☐	The claimant must have acted without carelessness.

The three elements make a claim for negligence possible. If the claimant has contributed to his injuries, damages may be reduced.

9   C   What is not reasonably foreseeable cannot be included in a claim *The Wagon Mound 1961*.

10   B   Answer A would not be enough care; answer D is too vague; answer C is too personalised.

---

3 English and alternative legal systems 3

1   C   The European Council sets EU strategy and policy.

2   C   This is the rule arising from *Donoghue v Stevenson 1932*.

3   Public, private, enabling, codifying.

4   B   Regulations of the European Union are not a form of delegated legislation; they come into automatic effect when issued. Acts of Parliament can be described as primary legislation; they are not delegated.

5   C   The most important element is proximity between the parties involved but there must also have been some foreseeable damage. In *Anns v Merton London Borough Council 1977* it was stated that the court must test whether there is sufficient proximity between the parties, such that the harm suffered was reasonably foreseeable.

6	D	*Obiter dicta* are never binding. *Ratio decidendi* (the statements of law behind decisions) can be binding in some certain instances.

7

- ☑ The person making the statement did so in an expert capacity of which the claimant was aware.
- ☑ The context in which the statement was made was such as to make it likely that the claimant would rely on it.
- ☑ In making the statement the defendant foresaw that it would be relied upon by the claimant.
- ☐ The claimant considered the statement.
- ☐ The claimant was not insured for financial loss.

The claimant must have actually relied on the statement; insurance is irrelevant.

8	D	The others are all civil cases.
9	A	Parliament may delegate the power to make legislation to local authorities, who thereby are allowed to make bye-laws, (i). If it is so provided in the enabling Act, delegated legislation may have to go through the 40-day 'laying before' procedure without a resolution against it before it comes into force, (iv). (ii) is incorrect since ministerial powers are exercised by statutory instrument. Orders in Council are an emergency, not a common, measure. (iii) is incorrect because Parliament may revoke enabling Acts.
10	D	Although an Act may rebut these presumptions by express words, they apply in the absence of any express provision to the contrary. (i) is incorrect since in fact the complete opposite is true – an Act applies to the whole of the UK unless it is specially expressed to exclude some part of it.

4 English and alternative legal systems 4

1	C	Indian law forms the basis of Sri Lanka's penal code.
2	B	Executive Orders and Agency Rules are forms of delegated legislation in the USA.
3	C	Criminal law is a type of public law.
4	B	The French court system is structured on these three levels.
5		Public, private, international, procedural.
6	A	Sejm is the lower house, Senate is the upper house. Sabah is a Malaysian court and Congress is found in the USA.
7	C	Binding norms are normal practice that have existed between nations for a long enough time to be seen as binding.
8	D	Judges under Sharia and codified systems can only apply the law. Judges under codified systems can be involved in judicial review to ensure the law is in line with certain principles such as a constitution.
9	B	In such circumstances, federal law prevails.

10		☑	Consumption of pork
		☑	Apostasy
		☑	Blasphemy
		☐	Mashtur
		☐	Madhab

Mashtur is a classification of the reliability of Ahadith, Madhab is a secondary source of Sharia law.

5 English and alternative legal systems 5

1	C	Comprehensibility and certainty are the two key principles of civil law.
2	B	Treaties and conventions are key sources of international law.
3	C	In France, tort is created by the Judiciary.
4	D	The House of Representatives consists of nationally elected members. The Senate consists of members elected regionally.

5		☑	Constitutional Acts
		☑	Acts of Parliament
		☐	Sharia law
		☑	Case law
		☑	Custom law

Sharia law is not a source of law in Denmark.

6	B	Judges do not make the law under such systems and it is the state that interprets international law, not its courts.
7	B	The traditional Chinese legal system can be traced back to the teachings of the important philosopher Confucius.
8	B	In the Russian legal system, disputes between businesses are heard by Courts of Arbitration.
9	A	Sharia law is explicitly based on the religion of Islam and governs all aspects of a believer's life, both moral and legal. Therefore A is a correct statement.
10	D	Acceptable is not one of the recognised categories. Note that the others are the Five Pillars of Islam according to CIMA's syllabus.

6 Establishing contractual obligations 1

1	C	The tort of deceit is only applicable to fraudulent misrepresentations.
2	B	A revocation is not actioned until received, whereas an acceptance is actioned as soon as it is sent. (The postal rule.)
3	D	Damages are available under the Misrepresentation Act 1967.

4	B	(i) is not good consideration as it is no more than one would be expected to do in the circumstances. (iii) is past consideration.
5	A	A request for service carries an implied duty to pay. The amount can be fixed later.
6	B	Revocation of an offer may be communicated by a reliable informant (*Dickinson v Dodds*) but communication of acceptance of an offer may only be made by a person actually authorised to do so: *Powell v Lee*. Hence Neil's brother's purported acceptance for Neil is invalid (Option D), but the lodger's communication of revocation to Neil is valid since his presence at the deal makes him a reliable informant (Option B). Tim's promise to keep the offer open was not supported by a separate option agreement and so he was free to sell before such time as he received acceptance (Option C). Since the offer was expressed to be kept open for a week, there is no question that Neil failed to accept within a reasonable time so that the offer lapsed (Option A).
7	D	The opposite is true.
8	C	That a price label, or even a display of goods, is an invitation to the customer to make an offer which the shop may then choose to accept. It is an invitation to treat (Option C).
9	B	Consideration need only be sufficient – it need not be adequate: *Thomas v Thomas*, (i). Performance of an existing contractual duty is not good consideration (iii) Consideration does not need to be provided at the time the contact is made as a promise to pay or provide a service is all that is required (iv) Hence only (ii) is correct – as consideration is the price of a promise, it must be paid by the person who seeks to enforce it: *Tweddle v Atkinson*.
10	D	Brian varied the terms of the offer when replying to Alexander.

7 Establishing contractual obligations 2

1	C	The others are invitations to treat. Do not confuse the auction itself (it is an invitation to treat) with a bid made at auction. A bid made is an offer to buy the item that is being auctioned.
2	C	The contract is valid unless set aside by the representee.
3	B	Promissory estoppel requires:

– A creditor promising a debtor that they will not insist on full discharge of the debt.
– The promise is unsupported by consideration.
– Intention that the debtor will act on the promise, and they do so.

The creditor is estopped from retracting the promise unless the debtor can be restored to their original position.

4	D	A promise to waive an existing right given for no consideration is not binding, and Miranda's payment of less than is due is not consideration for Emma's promise: *Foakes v Beer* (Option A). Emma would only be estopped from retracting her waiver if she had made it with the intention that Miranda should place reliance on it and Miranda then did so (Option B). In fact she made the promise because she needed cash. The fact that Miranda may or may not have taken advantage of Emma (Option C) is irrelevant. Hence, because she received no consideration and is not affected by promissory estoppel, Emma may claim the £100 balance (Option D).
5	A	Contracts may be oral or implied by conduct.

6	A	As C Ltd is not a party to the contract, A Ltd cannot sue C Ltd in the law of contract.
7	D	There has been no misrepresentation in this scenario.
8	B	The assumption is rebuttable, so the parties are free to try and prove that legal relations were not intended.
9	B	This is similar to the use of a telex in *Entores v Miles Far Eastern Corporation*. The offeree must make sure that his acceptance is understood when using any instantaneous method of communication.
10	B	Misrepresentation makes a contract voidable, but not void. The contract remains valid, and the representee may choose to affirm it.

8 Establishing contractual obligations 3

1	C	The three essential elements of contract are: offer and acceptance (ie agreement), consideration and intention to create legal relations. Some contracts require written terms, but by no means all.
2	C	Contracts for the sale of land must be completed by deed and are therefore specialty contracts.
3	D	Patrick's query is only a query as to whether other terms would be acceptable, that is, a request for information. Samantha responded to that request for information but her response is not a revocation of her original offer. As she has not revoked her offer, it is still open for Patrick to accept. This means that on Sunday, Patrick and Samantha have a contract.
4	C	Option B is wrong because consideration does not have to be adequate, but it does have to be sufficient. Option A is a red herring because the rent is sufficient consideration against the ongoing promise that Ben can stay. Option D is incorrect on its own. Consideration from Ben is required to enforce the promise: *Thomas v Thomas*.
5	C	Two offers do not constitute agreement, even if they say the same thing. Therefore Option A is wrong. Option D is nearly right. She must revoke her offer before Elizabeth **accepts** the offer, **not** before Elizabeth **receives** the letter. Option B is not right because the lack of agreement comes before the issue of consideration. If there had been agreement, consideration would have been in place (a necklace on one side and £250 on the other).
6	B	A representor must amend previous statements if what he has said has become misleading. This can be seen in *With v O'Flanagan*. It is an exception to the silence rule in Option A. Option C is irrelevant.
7	D	The presumption that commercial cases are legally binding is rebuttable if otherwise shown. Options A and B are wrong because the courts will presume commercial arrangements were intended to be legal. Option C is wrong because social or domestic arrangements are presumed not to have been intended to be legal.
8	D	Faxes are not subject to the postal rule. Per the rule in *Entores v Miles Far Eastern Corporation*, instantaneous methods of acceptance must be received.

| 9 | C | Revocation can be communicated by a reliable third party (as in *Dickinson v Dodds*). In this case, Dave can be seen as a reliable third party, because he has been involved in the process. Option A is wrong because the offer has been revoked. Option B is irrelevant as Lee has a right to revoke his offer at any time. Option D is wrong because Dave is a reliable third party. |
| 10 | A | A contract may be in any form unless a certain form is prescribed. Option B is wrong because consideration from each party does not have to be of equal value. Option C is wrong because contract is part of civil law. Option D is wrong because minors may not have contractual capacity to enter certain types of contract. |

9 Establishing contractual obligations 4

1	C	An illegal act cannot form the basis for a valid contract.
2	D	Lapse of time may act as a bar to rescission, but recission is in theory available for all types of misrepresentation.
3	B	An act the law requires in any case is not sufficient consideration. It is not necessarily past (the question did not specify) and it is not proper or sufficient by virtue of being insufficient.
4	B	Options A and C are executed consideration. Option D is past consideration.
5	D	The others are examples of contracts which must be in writing.
6	B	Option C is untrue, as verbal acceptance is valid if acknowledged. Option D is untrue as the £4,000 is consideration for the car.
7	D	It is presumed in social and domestic situations that legal relations are not intended and it is presumed in commercial situations that they are.
8	B	The misrepresentee may choose to affirm or repudiate the contract.
9	D	Standard form contracts are unlikely to be oral. Option C is wrong because the point of a standard contract is that it is set out by the stronger party, not negotiated by the parties.
10	B	Jude offers to buy and the till operator can accept or reject the offer.

10 Performing the contract 1

1	D	Breach of a warranty entitles the injured party to claim damages only.
2	D	The Sale of Goods Act 1979 implies terms concerning title, description, quality, fitness and sale by sample. Quantity and price are not covered.
3	C	The goods which are the subject of the contract must be for private use or consumption.
4	A	Title simply means legal ownership.
5	B	Breach of warranty does not cause the contract to be discharged. Terms implied by statute may be conditions.
6	B	A consumer must be a natural person, not acting for the purposes of trade.

7	B	*Poussard v Spiers; Bettini v Gye.*
		Failure to sing on an opening night breaks a condition of the contract. Missing rehearsals does not.
8	C	A warranty is a minor term in the contract. Breach of a minor term does not entitle the injured party to repudiate the contract. The injured party must continue with the contract, but may claim damages.
9	B	Generally in contract there is no rule that you must say what you know, but you must give a complete enough picture so as not to be misleading. Steve's answer may be true, but it is misleading because he hears his neighbour a lot, even if he doesn't see him, which makes him a bad neighbour. This is what Adam wanted to know. Similar to *Smith v Land and House Property Corporation.*
10	C	Judas has stated an opinion not a fact. This cannot be a misrepresentation. The facts in this case are similar to *Bisset v Wilkinson.*

11 Performing the contract 2

1	C	You should have spotted that (i) merely reiterates s 2(1) Unfair Contract Terms Act 1977 (UCTA) – an exclusion clause relating to death or personal injury is only void if it attempts to exclude liability arising from negligence. Where Wincey deals as a consumer, all the other clauses are void; a customer guarantee cannot limit liability for loss or damage (s 5 UCTA), the terms as to merchantable quality and fitness for purpose (s 14 Sale of Goods Act 1979 (SGA)) cannot be excluded and the product must comply with its description (s 13 SGA) by virtue of ss 6 and 7 UCTA. No supplier may exclude liability where he supplies goods to which he has no title (term implied by s 12 SGA): s 6(1) UCTA. But where Wincey does not deal as a consumer as defined by s 12 UCTA then only the exclusion clause as to title is void.
2	C	Option (i) is incorrect because some contracts (for example for land or shares) have a particular required form. Option (ii) is also wrong. Oral contracts are generally acceptable as they are.
3	C	Sian's representation was intended to form part of the contract.
4	A	This is the rule in s 2 of the Act.
5	A	Most contractual terms in business agreements are identified as being either conditions or warranties, (i) – the importance of the distinction being that failure to fulfil the former, (ii) leads to the whole contract being at an end (discharged by breach), whilst breach of warranty leads only to a claim for damages, not to discharge, (iii). An unclassified term as mentioned in (i) is one which cannot be identified as either a condition or warranty until the effects of failure to fulfil it are known and assessed. (iv) is incorrect since statute often implies warranties as well as conditions (for example Sale of Goods Act 1979).
6	A	Although a legally binding contract must be complete in its terms it is possible to look outside its express terms in order to fix a price so long as the method fixed is not uncertain.
7	B	The facts in this case are very similar to *Thompson v LMS Railway* where it was held that the conditions of carriage were adequately communicated in the train timetables and the exclusion clause was valid.

8	D	Most exclusion clauses aim either to restrict liability in the event of breach of contract or to limit the person's obligation to perform some or all of what he took on.
9	A	A representation is a statement of fact made before a contract is entered into. It is usually incorporated as a contractual term (condition or warranty) but it could still be a representation even if a contract is not ultimately formed. A representation is made with the intention that the other party should place reliance on it. Howard's statement is one of simple fact. It is not an extravagant claim and so cannot be said to be 'advertiser's puff'.
10	A	The requirement of the Act is fitness for purpose, ie the purpose for which it is bought, not all purposes. The others are genuine requirements of the Act.

12 Performing the contract 3

1	C	Liability for death and personal injury due to negligence can never be excluded.
2	D	The Act provides that the purpose behind the purchase must be given to the seller. If it is obvious (as might be assumed with a coat) the reason does not have to be given. However, if there is a peculiarity associated with the purchase (and in this case, an allergy would count as a peculiarity), the buyer must intimate that to the seller.
3	C	While if a description is applied to the goods by the contract, it is a sale by description, it is not the case that all descriptive words used form part of the contract terms.
4	B	In the case of *R&B Customs Brokers Co Ltd v United Dominions Trust Ltd 1988* a company was held to be a consumer when purchasing a company car as car dealing was not its trade.
		Under UTCCR 1999 a consumer contract cannot exclude protection under the Sale of Goods Act. Therefore the exclusion clause is not allowed.
5	A	Rescission entails setting aside a contract as if it had never been made.
6	C	It is not the case that a buyer must be explicit. He may specify the particular purpose quite broadly, as in *Ashington Piggeries v Christopher Hill Ltd.*
7	C	Literally this phrase translated means 'against he who is relying'. Anything ambiguous in an exclusion clause is interpreted against the person who is seeking to rely on it.
8	B	Statute can imply a term either by overriding an express term (for example the Sale of Goods Act 1979) or by providing a term which applies unless overridden (for example the Partnership Act 1890). The latter method is also the way in which custom and trade practice imply terms. In order to give 'business efficacy' to an agreement which is only deficit because the parties have failed to provide expressly for something because it was so obvious, the court may also imply terms: *The Moorcock.* But the court will not imply a term to provide for events not anticipated at the time of agreement, (iii), to contradict an express term, (iv) nor to remedy a defective agreement.
9	C	The scenario is similar to *Curtis v Chemical Cleaning Co,* where the claimant was misled as to the extent of the exclusion clause. This is an exception to the rule that once a document is signed, the person who signed is bound by any exclusion clauses contained therein.
10	D	The fact that the party is informing the other in advance of the date of contract makes his actions 'anticipatory'.

13 Performing the contract 4

1	A	The answer is not Option C because although statement (ii) is generally correct, there are exceptions to this rule, for example, if the person has been misled about the contents of the document.
2	B	The other options could potentially all be true. It is important to look at the timing of actions in the question to establish that Option B is the correct answer.
3	C	Option A is generally true unless there is intervention by a third party. Option B is untrue. In Option D, the fact that Kathleen is John's relative is irrelevant to her contracting with Catherine, as she is not Catherine's relative.
4	C	Breach of a warranty does not destroy a contract as it is only a minor term. However, the injured party is entitled to damages.
5	A	Option C is wrong, because breach of a condition entitles the injured party to repudiate. Option D is wrong by the same reason.
6	A	Some exclusions are valid in non-consumer contracts.
7	D	By the rule in *Pinnel's* case, as Grace has paid the part payment earlier than the due date, she has provided Rebecca with consideration for the waiver of Rebecca's rights.
8	B	A breach of warranty gives rise to damages only.
9	D	The scenario is similar to *Olley v Marlborough Court*.
10	D	The contra proferentem rule means that the courts rule against the person seeking to rely. A literal translation of the Latin is 'against the one relying'.

14 Contractual breakdown 1

1	A	Such a breach can automatically discharge a contract – but the party who is not at fault has an option to continue the contract until breach actually occurs.
2	D	This is not an exception in itself. The exception arises when the promise accepts partial performance.
3	C	Anticipatory breach or repudiation occurs when one party, expressly or by implication, indicates that he does not intend to be bound by an agreement. The injured party is entitled to sue immediately, though he may elect to allow the contract to continue until there is actual breach: *Hochster v De La Tour*. Because the right to sue is instantaneous, the injured party need not complete his obligations nor wait a reasonable time in order to effect his intentions.
4	D	Penalty clauses are void in contract law.
5	C	Option A is wrong because disinclination to perform the contract would represent a breach. Option B is wrong because the event must be central to the purpose of the contract for non-occurrence to cause frustration. Option D is wrong because increased expense is not a cause of frustration.

6	C	Consideration need not be adequate. Option B is nearly right. The courts will presume in the first instance that legal relations were not intended between man and wife, but the presumption is rebuttable. In this case, the facts that Rosie and Jim are separated, the agreement is about property and is in writing would in all probability lead the court to presume legal relations were intended, as in *Merritt v Merritt*.
7	B	Damages are a common law remedy. Option D is incorrect because it actually describes an equitable order of specific performance.
8	A	The scenario in this question is similar to that in *Hadley v Baxendale*. The loss must have been reasonably foreseeable to the defendant for damages to be awarded.
9	B	The general rule of privity of contract states that only a person who is party to a contract has enforceable obligations under it. Hence, Options A and C are wrong because F is not a party to the contract and Option D is wrong because Dee is a party to the contract.
10	A	The debt must be acknowledged by the debtor in writing. This acknowledgement must be signed by the debtor.

15 Contractual breakdown 2

1	C	The limitation in Option C applies to the claimant not the defendant. The limitation period begins to run when the claimant's disability ceases or he dies.
2	C	*Quantum meruit* is a common law remedy.
3	A	An injunction will not be made merely to restrain acts inconsistent with the contract's obligation.
4	D	In *Hotel Services v Hilton International 2000*, loss of profit was considered direct in identical circumstances.
5	C	Damages generally seek to place the injured party in the position he would have been in had the contract been performed. Only sometimes are damages paid to cover expenses that have arisen as part of the breached contract.
6	D	Frustration occurs where the contract becomes fundamentally different from what was expected, or becomes impossible. It does not occur when assumptions are not proved correct.
7	B	Options C and D are wrong because the point of civil law is to compensate the injured party, not to punish the wrongdoer. The result in Option A would be achieved by an equitable remedy such as quantum meruit.
8	D	Horatio was within the terms of the contract in not loading the waste onto the ship within 28 days of arrival. Had he informed Rodney that he had no intention of ever loading the waste, there would have been anticipatory breach. However, as Rodney had not taken action against him, the frustrating event would have overridden the breach anyway. The contract is frustrated by supervening illegality.
9	D	A contract is not discharged by frustration if there is an alternative method of carrying out the contract, albeit a more expensive method. The facts in this scenario were similar to *Tsakiroglou & Co v Noblee and Thorl GmbH*.

10   C   Where the agreement states that a fixed sum is to be payable this will become due only when precise, exact and complete performance has been rendered. Failure in this respect will not entitle the person to part payment (Option C). Where one party prevents complete performance (Option A) the other may claim part payment by way of quantum meruit: *Planché v Colburn*. A divisible contract (where payment is to be made by instalments) requires that separate payment be made for each tranche or work (Option D). The doctrine of substantial performance (Option B) states that where work has been completed but a small number of deficiencies remain the contractor is entitled to payment less a deduction (or retention) to cover the cost of the outstanding work: *Hoenig v Isaacs*.

16 Contractual breakdown 3

1   C   An order for specific performance would not be made for a contract of personal service because the court would not be able to ensure that a person complied fully with the order.

2   A   In Option A, fundamental breach allows the injured party either to accept the other party's offer that the contract be discharged or reject it. In the latter case the contract remains in force, the injured party continues with his obligations and his remedy is to sue for damages for any loss caused by the other person's actions. Option C is incorrect because he may claim damages for breach as well as for loss following his continued performance. Option D is incorrect because either cause to claim damages is independent of an injunction.

3   D   Specific performance is an equitable remedy.

4   C   *Quantum meruit* literally means 'how much it is worth'.

5   B   Mark is entitled to sue for breach of contract due to the non-delivery. However, he will only recover limited damages as he should have accepted cash on delivery when he was offered it. The scenario in the question is similar to *Payzu Ltd v Saunders*.

6   C   Options A and B are not correct as Robina has been prevented from performing by History Alive. Option D is not right because the fact that one of the parties has cancelled the series is not a frustrating event, it is the other party breaching the contract.

7   C   Option A is not right, because the fact that the fixed sum of damages arranged covers several issues implies that it is a penalty clause rather than a genuine pre-estimate of loss. If the pre-arranged sum is judged to be a penalty clause, then the clause is void.

8   B   Option C is a description of a penalty clause. Option D is a description of damages to cover wasted expenditure. Option A was a red herring. In some instances parties lodge money with the court prior to court action. However, you should have recognised the description of liquidated damages in Option B.

9   B   To be a frustrating event, the event which is not occurring must have been the whole purpose of the contract.

10   A   Option D is wrong because if the problem is caused by one of the parties it cannot be frustration. Options B and C are wrong because increases in expense or difficulty do not amount to frustration either.

17 Contractual breakdown 4

1 D Because frustration of a contract of personal service, such as an employment contract, occurs when the person is incapable of performance, this will clearly arise where the employee is too ill to work: *Condor v Barron Knights*. It will also be the case when he is dead, in prison or absent on military service (either in the UK or abroad). However, the contract of employment is not frustrated by the outbreak of war, (v). Instead it is rendered void since no person can continue to have contractual relations with an enemy alien.

2 B This accounts for the expectations of the parties to the contract. Options C and D are red herrings. Option A describes reliance interest.

3 A Rupert has performed the contract substantially, he is entitled to payment, but Davina may withhold the costs of the minor corrections; *Hoenig v Isaacs*.

4 B Under the rule in *Victoria Laundry (Windsor) v Newman Industries*, Whin Mechanics could not have known about the lucrative contract. Therefore they are not liable for the exceptional profits.

5 D This is correct according to the rule in *H Parsons (Livestock) v Uttley Ingham*.

6 C The courts will often use the remedy of specific performance in cases of land transfer. A contract to pay money to a third party could be enforced by specific performance. However, an order for specific performance is never used for contracts of employment as performance would be required over time and the courts could not be sure that performance would be maintained.

7 D Botch Job have substantially performed the contract in that Belinda has a new bathroom on the first floor. However, Belinda may retain the cost of righting small defects in the job.

8 D *Tsakiroglu & Co v Noble and Thorl Gmbh.* The other three are frustrating events: *Taylor v Caldwell* (A), *Condor v Barron Knights* (B) and *Avery v Bowden* (C).

9 C An order for specific performance (B) is an equitable remedy, which would not be appropriate here. Tee Ltd can expect to reclaim the amount needed to put the company in the position it would have been in if the contract had been performed.

10 B The rule in *Anon 1495* means that if alternative consideration is given in the form of goods, then waiver of a debt is valid. Option D is irrelevant. In Option C, the consideration of a dress may not be adequate, but it is sufficient. The bargain does not have to be good.

18 Employment 1

1 D The duty to provide work is implied only in certain circumstances.

2

☐	Employees of any age may be eligible to claim
✓	There is no qualifying period
✓	There is frequently no limit on the amount of compensation that a tribunal can award
☐	Claims must be made within three months of the dismissal
✓	Employees taking part in unofficial strike action are protected from unfair dismissal

Generally there is a qualifying period of a year, and compensation is capped by the Employment Rights Act 1996. Those on official, not unofficial, strike action are protected.

3	D	Breach of Health and Safety is a criminal offence.
4	C	Dismissal for membership of a trade union is not allowed by statute.
5	D	Although summary dismissal on liquidation is a breach of contract which can be treated as wrongful dismissal, Deck Line Ltd's liquidator is allowed to justify his action by reliance on evidence uncovered after the event (which is not the situation with unfair dismissal). Hence Mick's dishonesty justifies Deck Line Ltd's action.
6	C	Options A and B are untrue. Option D is wrong because it is sometimes permissible for the new employer to vary the terms of employment if there are economic, technical or organisational reasons to do so.
7	C	Option A is clearly dismissal as the employer has expressly requested the employer to leave. Option B is constructive dismissal. In Option D, failure to renew a fixed term contract is also dismissal.
8	A	Protection is provided by Race Relations Act 1976, Disability Discrimination Act 1995 and Sex Discrimination Act 1975.
9	B	The mobility clause is a contractual term.
10	D	Only the employee would rank as a preferential creditor. The contractor would be an ordinary creditor.

19 Employment 2

1	C	Options A and B are unlikely due to the breakdown in confidence between the parties. D only would be awarded if Options A or B had been awarded and the employer had ignored the order.
2	C	The employer can withhold wages.
3	B	You should have recognised the other tests. Documentation may help to establish answers to the other tests.
4	A	Where an employer has taken all reasonable steps to prevent an accident they should not be found liable.
5	B	An employee who has worked more than one month but less than two years is entitled to a minimum of a week's notice. When an employee has worked somewhere for two years, they are entitled to a week's notice for each full year of continuous employment.
6	A	This statement is untrue. Independent contractors are paid gross of tax. The others are all valid reasons.
7	D	The duty to provide work is only true in certain circumstances.
8	B	In the others being male is a genuine occupational qualification. In England, such custom is overridden by statute.
9	C	There is no duty to provide references, although most employers do so.
10	C	The others are genuine rules. An employee working under separate contracts for the same employer may not aggregate his hours, however.

20 Employment 3

1 C All the people in Options A, B and D are entitled to be employees.

2 C Terms may be implied by a collective agreement between the union and the employer if they satisfy three conditions: if they are a custom 'reasonable, certain and notorious' in the industry, known to the employee and a negotiated agreement.

3 D The employee only has an implied duty of obedience to reasonable commands. The employer can be protected from the situations outlined in Options A and B. Option C is untrue because the employer has no duty to give references.

4 B While claims for wrongful dismissal can be heard in the courts, claims for unfair dismissal must be heard by the tribunal. Thus, due to the wording of the question, Option B is the right answer.

5 A Option B is only true if the employee has been made redundant.

6 A Summary dismissal may not be a breach of contract, for example, if it was for misconduct. The others imply breach of contract. Constructive dismissal is when an employee feels their contract has been breached, wrongful dismissal is a breach of contract, and if the employer terminates through inability, it is still a breach of contract on his part.

7 B Employers usually provide tools and equipment, and they are obliged to deduct income tax from an employee's wages.

8 B Employers are liable for tortious acts as well as criminal acts of employees except where the act was made by the employee independent of the employer.

9 A There is no common law duty to provide a reference.

10 A Striking can be a fair reason for dismissal, as can being a threat to national security and legal prohibitions.

21 Employment 4

1 C Members of the armed forces (A) are excluded from much legislation on grounds of national security; those employed outside Great Britain would not be subject to UK law and strike action can be a fair reason for dismissal.

2 D In the past, wrongful dismissal was always heard in the courts. Now the jurisdiction of the employment tribunal has been extended to include wrongful dismissal.

3 C The employee cannot be expected never to make mistakes. Only reasonable competence is required. Options B and D are also implied duties of the employee.

4 A The others are examples of the few circumstances where racial discrimination is permitted.

5 B The written particulars must give reference to where the rules on health and safety can be found.

6 C She is entitled to the statutory minimum notice period, which in this case is ten weeks (one for each year of her employment).

7	B	He would have been entitled had he been made redundant.
8	D	These are all potentially fair reasons for dismissal.
9	B	Because the statue only recommends the wearing of goggles it does not of itself create a statutory duty and so on this point Kay Michael Ltd will not be liable to Roger, (i). It is open to Kay Michael Ltd to raise the defence of reasonable care, (ii) though it is unlikely to succeed given the location of the goggles and the notice, and the attitude of the foreman. An employer cannot raise the defence that the employee consented to a dangerous working practice (iii). Finally it is clear that the company is in breach of its common law duty as regards a safe system of work, (iv).
10	D	Dismissal occurs when a fixed term contract is not renewed, even though such an eventuality is implicit in the fact that the agreement has a fixed term. Nick is therefore entitled to claim for redundancy pay and/or compensation for unfair dismissal if he can prove the requisite facts. However, non-renewal cannot give rise to a claim for wrongful dismissal, which is only possible when there has been summary dismissal or dismissal with less than the required period of notice.

22 Company formation 1

1
- ✓ Cannot offer its shares or debentures to the public
- ✓ Cannot allow its shareholders to offer their shares direct to the public
- ☐ Must have a minimum of two members, otherwise the sole member may become personally liable for the debts of the company
- ✓ Cannot be registered with a name which is the same as that of an existing registered company
- ☐ Must have at least two directors

A private company may be formed and operate with only one member and one director.

2	D	The 15% applies to minority protection in cases of variation of class rights, not of all the articles.
3	C	Public companies are not permitted to trade until they have received a Certificate of Incorporation and a Trading Certificate.
4	A	A special resolution is required.
5	D	A public company must have at least two directors and a secretary. It must also have at least one member.
6	A	A company cannot enforce a contract before it comes into existence (Option C), and cannot ratify a pre-incorporation contract (Option A). The promoters may be liable (Option B): s 51(1).
7	B	Word 'limited' can be omitted if the company promotes art, commerce, science, education, religion, charity or any profession, and the profits are applied to promoting them.

8   ☑ A memorandum of association

☐ Articles of association

☑ A statement of the first directors and secretary

☑ A statutory declaration of compliance with the requirements of the Companies Act

☐ A register of members

A company need not submit its own articles; it can instead state that it is adopting model articles and not submit any. A register of members is not required to register a company.

9   B   Third parties to such contracts are protected by ss 39 and 40.

10   D   *Eley v Positive Government Security Assurance Co Ltd* illustrates that the statutory rules only apply to rights as a shareholder, and not rights of shareholders who are suing in another capacity.

23 Company formation 2

1   A   A company has a separate legal identity: *Salomon v Salomon Ltd*.

2   ☐ The register of directors' residential addresses

☑ The register of members

☑ Copies of directors' service contracts

☐ The register of debentureholders

☑ Register of charges

The register of directors' residential addresses must be kept but it is not generally available to members. Companies are not legally required to keep a register of debentureholders.

3   C   A company limited by guarantee, a single member private company and a corporation sole are legitimate artificial legal persons.

4

Statement	True	False
A director's service address can be the company's registered office.	✓	
Directors' service contracts must be made available for inspection by the general public.		✓
The register of members contains among other things the names and addresses of each member.	✓	
A company does not legally have to keep a register of debentureholders.	✓	

A director may give his service address as the company's registered office for the purposes of the register of directors. Only members can inspect copies of directors' service contracts. The names and addresses of members are included on the register of members and a company does not have to keep a register of debentureholders although in practice most do.

| 5 | A | The capital available is below the lower limit for a plc (Option B). They wish to protect their other assets, so should not form an unlimited company (Option D). They cannot be shareholders and give a guarantee (Option C). |

6

- ✓ Sign and file accounts
- ✓ Appoint auditors if appropriate
- ☐ Notify the Registrar of any qualifications held by the members
- ✓ Notify the Registrar when a member leaves
- ☐ Submit a copy of the partnership agreement to the Registrar

Notification of member qualifications and submission of the partnership agreement are not requirements. The filing of accounts, appointment of auditors where appropriate and notification when a member leaves are.

7	B	Any alteration must benefit the company as a whole. Court approval is not required.
8	B	Answers A, C and D all relate to the period prior to incorporation, when the company does not exist and therefore cannot be party to an agreement.
9	C	There is no partnership between a shopkeeper and employee and as Joe is liable for the business' debts, it is not a company.
10	A	The original members will be the formation agents, and when the company is purchased, the purchasers will want to become members themselves. None of the other changes is compulsory, though in practice all would generally occur.

24 Company formation 3

1	D	The nominal value of allotted share capital must be £50,000.
2	A	Option B is untrue; a director can do this (and has: *Lee v Lee's Air Farming*). Option C is a true statement, but is governed by the Insolvency Act 1986, not Salomon's case. Option D is untrue – this is essentially what Mr Salomon had done, and the transaction was valid.
3	C	A public company has six months to file accounts, a private company has nine.
4	B	A special resolution is required per s 21. Extraordinary resolutions do not exist under the Companies Act 2006.
5	C	Liability is limited to the guaranteed amount, and is due only in the event of liquidation.

6

- ✓ The ability to sue in the business's name
- ✓ The ability to mortgage the business's assets
- ☐ The treatment of the brothers' income from the business for tax purposes
- ☐ The ability to create a floating charge over the business's assets
- ✓ The brothers' rights to participate in the management of the business

Although a partnership is not a separate legal entity, it can sue in its own name as a legal convenience. A partnership can grant a mortgage or fixed charge over a specific item of property but cannot create a floating charge. The brothers retain their right to participate in the management of the business. Directors are taxed through the PAYE system. Partners receive untaxed drawings and must account for tax on the partnership's profit at the end of the year.

7	B	Model articles shall be provided automatically.
8	A	Unrestricted objects reduces the possibility of *ultra vires* contracts.
9	A	*Eley v Positive Government Security Life Assurance Co.*

9 A   The articles are a contract between a company and its members in their capacity as members.

10
✓	There are at least two partners.
☐	There must be an intention to trade.
✓	There must be some form of business activity.
✓	Partners are agents of the partnership.
☐	Partners are only liable for contracts they personally signed.

There must be an intention to make profit, not just to trade. All partners are jointly liable for the firm's debts.

25 Company formation 4

1	B	The Companies Act allows a private company to be formed and operate with one member; no secretary is needed.
2	B	A company cannot be liable on a pre-incorporation contract as the company does not exist at the time the contract is made.
3	A	The company owns it own property.
4	B	The other options are all situations where a court will 'lift the veil'.

5

Statement	True	False
The articles of association sets out the regulations governing the internal conduct of the company.	✓	
The articles of association are registered with the registrar of companies after the registrar has issued a certificate of incorporation.		✓
The articles of association are required for a public company, but not for a private company.		✓
The articles of association must state the company's name.	✓	

The articles set out the company's regulations. They are registered before incorporation, by both public and private companies, and contain the company's name.

| 6 | C | *Ultra vires* means literally: outside the powers. |

7		
	☐	A £20 registration fee.
	☑	The registered office address.
	☑	The name of the LLP.
	☑	The names and addresses of all the members.
	☐	A copy of the partnership agreement.

The registration fee is £95. The partnership agreement is not required.

8   B   If Crawley rescinds (Option A), then it won't have the antique which it is contractually bound to sell to Broadfield for a profit of £5,000 and Broadfield will sue it. It will lose £2,500 profit if it does nothing (Option D). Option C would be correct if Crawley had paid the money to Charles; as the company has not done so, the simplest solution is to pay Charles the cost price and leave him with no legal remedy.

9   C   A public company must have a quarter of its nominal value paid up, so Option D is incorrect. It must have a share capital of at least £50,000 nominal value so Options A and B are incorrect.

10   C   A member or members must hold a minimum of 15% of the company's issued share capital.

26 Company formation 5

1

Statement	True	False
Alterations may compel a member to subscribe for additional shares.		✓
Alterations are void if they conflict with the Companies Act.	✓	
A person cannot obtain an injunction to prevent the alteration of articles where the alteration affects their contract contained within it.	✓	
An alteration may be deemed void if it can be proved that the majority who passed it were not acting bona fide in the interests of the company as a whole.	✓	

A member cannot be compelled to subscribe for additional shares.

2   A   The alteration is not a fraud on the minority (Option B). Shareholders voting on an alteration of the articles must vote in the best interests of the company: *Greenhalgh v Arderne Cinemas*, so Option C is incorrect. There is no infringement of statutory rights (Option D).

3   A   A private company must keep accounting records for three years.

4   ☑ A public company has six months from the end of its accounting period to produce and file its annual accounts; a private company has nine months.

☑ A company limited by guarantee can only be a private company; it cannot be a public company.

☐ The Companies Act rule that ordinary shares allotted for cash must be first offered to members applies to public, not private, companies.

☑ Under the Companies Act, private companies do not have to hold an AGM.

☐ A private company must have at least one member, public companies must have two.

Pre-emption rights apply to both types of company and both may have a single member.

5   D   Companies have 28 days to file their annual return.

6   C   Injunctions can prevent a company from doing something. In this case from using another's registered name.

7   C   The director has a duty to abide by the constitution of the company and has clearly breached it (s171).

8   D   The approval of the relevant class of members must be obtained.

9   A   A company's constitution binds the company and its members.

10   D   The certificate of incorporation is conclusive proof of the date the company was formed.

27 Company formation 6

1

Statement	True	False
A private limited company is a company which has not registered under the Companies Act to be a public company.	✓	
A private limited company is an incorporated business.	✓	
A private limited company is not required by law to file annual accounts at Companies House.		✓
The shareholders of a private company cannot benefit from limited liability.		✓

A private company is any company that is not a public company. It is incorporated. All limited companies must file accounts. A private limited company is so called because shareholders' liability is limited.

2   D   A public company must obtain a trading certificate before it can do anything.

3   A   The business would have to be called Lynn plc if it was a public limited company (Option B). A sole trader cannot state that it is limited (Option C), and the company is stated as being limited, not unlimited (Option D).

4   A   The London Gazette is used to publish legal notices.

5   D   *Adams v Cape Industries* emphasises that companies within groups should generally be treated as separate legal entities.

6	B	The certificate of incorporation is conclusive evidence of the date and fact of incorporation.

7

- ☑ No requirement to file accounts
- ☑ All the profit accrues to the owner
- ☐ The business is liable for all business debts
- ☑ More control over the business than a company
- ☐ Easier to raise finance

The owner is liable for the business debts. Sole traders often find it hard to raise finance.

8	B	See *Gilford Motor Co v Horne*.
9	D	Model articles automatically apply to all companies limited by shares, but there are different models for different types of company.
10	C	(iv) is incorrect as the Combined Code is not legally binding.

28 Company administration and management 1

1	B	Where directors exceed their powers the company may be liable on contracts with third parties.
2	C	An ordinary resolution with special notice is required.
3	A	Shareholders holding at least 95% of the company's shares must agree.
4	C	A special resolution is required to alter the articles.
5	D	A public company secretary is required to have qualifications. Every public company is required to have a company secretary. A company secretary can bind the company in some contracts: *Panorama Developments (Guildford) Ltd v Fidelis Furnishing Fabrics Ltd* but not if they act outside their actual or apparent authority.

6

- ☑ The alteration of the articles of association
- ☑ The appointment of a director
- ☐ The removal of an auditor
- ☑ Reduction of share capital
- ☐ The removal of a director

Auditors and directors have the right to speak at a meeting concerning their removal so a meeting must be held at which a vote is taken.

7

- ☐ Where the articles provide a quorum of one for a general meeting, and the company is not a single member company
- ☑ A board meeting
- ☑ Where a meeting is held by order of the court
- ☑ A class meeting where all the shares are held by one member
- ☐ Where a meeting of five members is convened but only one turns up

The articles cannot override the principle that a meeting cannot consist of only one person, though the court can. A private company's board may only consist of a single director and the shareholder class may only consist of a single member, so in both cases one would be a valid quorum.

8	A	Members must hold 5% of the share capital or voting rights.
9	D	Directors have a duty under s 177 to declare an interest in a proposed transaction with the company.
10	C	Members are part of the company and are entitled to inspect the minutes or demand copies.

29 Company administration and management 2

1	B	*Bushell v Faith*
2	D	This is still counted as obtaining a personal advantage through being a director.

3

- ☑ Promote the success of the company
- ☐ Promote the relationship between directors and employees
- ☐ Declare trading losses to the stock exchange
- ☑ Declare an interest in an existing transaction or arrangement
- ☑ Exercise reasonable judgement

See ss 172, 174 and 182.

4

Statement	True	False
The articles may authorise anything that might otherwise be a breach of statutory duty.	✓	
Directors will not be liable for breaching statutory conflict of interest rules if they follow any lawful provisions for dealing with them contained in the articles.	✓	
Articles may normally permit less onerous regulations than the Companies Act.		✓
Some conflicts of interest by independent directors are permissible by the articles.	✓	

Articles may not normally permit less onerous regulations unless in the exceptional circumstances listed in the other options.

5	A	In the absence of a quorum fixed by the articles or directors, it is however deemed to be two.
6	C	The notice required is 21 days, not 28.
7	C	If directors use their powers irregularly to allot shares, the votes attached to the new shares may not be used in reaching a decision in general meeting to sanction it: *Howard Smith Ltd v Ampol Petroleum Ltd*.
8	C	A plc must hold its AGM within six months of its accounting reference date. It has already held its AGM for 20X6 accounts and therefore the next accounting reference date is 31 July 20X7. Six months after is 31 January 20X8.

9   D   Directors of a plc must call a general meeting if the company's net assets fall to half or less of its called-up share capital.

10   D   Proxies have the same rights as the members they represent.

30 Company administration and management 3

1   A   Two members or proxies are required.

2   C   The Act sets out the short notice requirements which need to be followed here because adequate notice has not been given.

3   B   A special resolution is needed to change the articles, requiring 75 votes at least, not more than 75 votes. Thus 25 votes (Option A) will not be enough to defeat the resolution. 50 votes (Option C) would be needed to defeat an ordinary resolution (where the vote needed in favour is more than 50%.)

4

Statement	True	False
Liability may arise through lifting the veil of incorporation.	✓	
Directors can never be liable to a company's creditors.		✓
A limited company may by special resolution provide that its directors have unlimited liability for its debts.	✓	
Directors are generally liable for the acts of the other directors.		✓

Directors can be liable to a company's creditors in certain circumstances but are not generally liable for the acts of other directors.

5   D   Any one member, regardless of their shareholding, can apply.

6   B   *Daniels v Daniels*

7   D   The transaction is not voidable because there has been sufficient disclosure elsewhere. The auditors have a statutory duty to remedy disclosure deficiencies but need not resign.

8
- ☐ Every year one third of directors should retire.
- ☑ At the first AGM all the directors should retire.
- ☑ Directors in office longest since their last election shall be retired.
- ☐ The question of who is to retire may be decided by lot.
- ☑ Retiring directors are eligible for re-election.

One half should retire and they may be re-elected. Lots may be used but are not always needed.

9   B   Only private companies may make written resolutions.

10   D   Written resolutions cannot be used to remove a director, so Option A is incorrect. Auditors must be sent copies of written resolutions, but have no right of objection (Option B). Written resolutions can be used notwithstanding any provisions in the company's articles, so Option C is incorrect.

31 Company administration and management 4

1   B   Only one director need be a natural person.

2   C   Special notice must be given to the company in respect of resolutions to remove directors and auditors.

3   C   21 days notice is required.

4   B   *Ebrahimi v Westbourne Galleries*.

5   B   Benefits of derivative actions accrue to the company only.

6   C   Directors do not have a responsibility to individual shareholders but to the company. D is incorrect as a dividend is only paid if there are funds available and the directors decide to do so. C is correct. Past directors owe duties regarding conflicts of interest and accepting benefits from third parties.

7   A   21 days and 50% (Option B) are the figures for an ordinary resolution proposed at an annual general meeting.

8   B   Under the Company Directors Disqualification Act 1986 a director must be disqualified if he is unfit to be concerned in the management of a company. This is for a minimum of two years and a maximum of fifteen years depending on how serious the offence was.

9   D   The remuneration of the director is irrelevant.

10

☑	Managing directors
☑	Chairmen
☑	Non-executive directors
☐	Advisers without board positions
☐	All involved in the management of a company

The Companies Act regulations apply only to members of the board.

32 Company administration and management 5

1   C   The articles cannot exempt directors from liability.

2

☑	Ensure the functions of the board are carried out.
☑	Provide an agenda.
☐	Distribute any paperwork.
☑	Ensure the meeting proceeds efficiently.
☐	Arrange a suitable location.

The secretary would distribute the paperwork and arrange the location.

3   A   Only 5% is needed for private companies that have not held a meeting for twelve months or more.

4   Executive, non-executive, managing, shadow.

5	D	Inquorate meetings are adjourned.
6	D	Private limited companies are not required to hold an AGM.
7	C	A shareholder is not sufficiently connected.
8	C	Under s 177 the nature and extent of the transaction must be disclosed to the members and directors.
9	A	*Dorchester Finance Co Ltd v Stebbing*.
10	A	Auditors have the right to attend general meetings only.

33 Corporate finance 1

1	A	B is a description of a floating charge.
2	B	A company can use the money it receives from share issues to trade and perhaps make losses and become insolvent.
3	C	S 561 sets out the general rule which applies unless otherwise sanctioned in general meeting.
4	C	S 656. 28 days notice is required.

5

☐ Pass an ordinary resolution with the usual notice
☑ Pass a special resolution with the usual notice
☑ Obtain permission of the court
☑ Produce a solvency statement
☐ Amend the statement of Capital and Initial Shareholdings

Private companies must pass a special resolution with usual notice, and obtain court permission or produce a solvency statement. An alteration of the statement of capital is not required to enable the reduction. It would be amended once the reduction has been completed.

6	C	Option D is incorrect since unincorporated organisations cannot create floating charges as they have no separate legal existence.

7

Statement	True	False
Returning capital to the holders of preference shares		✓
Issuing a new class of preference share with priority over an existing class of ordinary share		✓
Reduction of voting rights attached to a class of share	✓	
Issuing shares of a particular class of share to allottees who are not already members of that class		✓

See *House of Fraser plc v ACGE Investments Ltd*, *Re John Smith's Tadcaster Brewery Co Ltd* and *White v Bristol Aeroplane Co Ltd*.

8	D	Authority can be granted by ordinary resolution, a special resolution or a provision in the articles.
9	A	Only private companies may give assistance.
10	A	The share premium account may be used to pay for the costs of new share issues.

34 Corporate finance 2

1	B	112,500 – 90,000 – 10,000 + 5,000. Option A is the maximum amount that a public company could distribute. The share premium account is an undistributable reserve, so Option C is wrong.
2	A	Charges rank in the order of their creation, but fixed charges take precedence over floating charges unless the charges themselves state otherwise.
3	D	No company can issue shares at a discount: (Option A). A public company's shares can at minimum be a quarter paid up: (Option B). A public company is prohibited from accepting an undertaking to do work or perform services: (Option (C).

4

Statement	True	False
The directors will always be liable to recompense the company's creditors.		✓
The directors may be liable to recompense the company's creditors.	✓	
The members will always be liable to recompense the company's creditors.		✓
The members will never be liable to recompense the company's creditors.	✓	

The directors may be liable if found guilty of fraudulent or wrongful trading, or if the articles state that they have unlimited liability, but they are not automatically liable. Unsteady Ltd is a limited liability company, hence its members will only be liable for the amounts unpaid on their shares.

5	C	Fraud is not the same thing as a mistake (Option B). The court cannot override the decision of the Registrar (Option D), and the certificate is valid and conclusive evidence that the charge was registered properly within the appropriate time period (Option A).
6	A	Although the articles may also give the rights listed in Options B to D.

7
- ☑ Power to do so must be included in the Articles
- ☑ The company must pass a special resolution
- ☑ The company must obtain the confirmation of the court or issue a statement of solvency to proceed with the scheme
- ☐ The company must obtain written authorisation by its auditor
- ☐ The Registrar must be informed

The first three requirements must be met. Auditor authorisation is not required, the Registrar would be notified after the reduction has been completed.

8	A	A receiver cannot be appointed if an administration order is already in place. Only a floating charge holder is entitled to place the company in administration. Debenture holders receive interest payments not dividends.
9	D	A special resolution is required S 716.
10	D	The purpose is to consider the steps that should be taken to deal with the situation.

35 Corporate finance 3

1	B	A is a description of a fixed charge.
2	C	Registration must occur within 21 days.
3		✓ Redemption of redeemable shares ✓ Purchase of shares under the reduction of capital procedures ✓ Purchase of shares in compliance with a court order ☐ Purchase of own shares if a shareholder has made a bid for 90% of the issue share capital ☐ Purchase of own shares by a quoted company
4	B	The company has a duty to pay interest on the debentures based on the contract under which they were formed. There is, however, no necessity for the company to pay a dividend to ordinary shareholders; a decision not to do so is within the company's discretion. A debentureholder (whether or not secured by a charge over the company assets) is a creditor of the company (not a member) and therefore takes precedence in a liquidation (Option D).
5	B	Members and creditors cannot reclaim unlawful dividends.
6	A	Private companies can disapply the rights permanently by provisions in their articles.
7	C	A return must be made within 28 days.
8	D	Options A, B and C are defined as undistributable.
9	C	15% and 21 days is the requirement.
10	C	Company law lays down certain rules regarding the register if it is kept, but does not require it to be kept.

36 Corporate finance 4

1	B	Debentures can be issued at a discount but shares cannot.
2	B	Only the remaining issued capital may be called up, not all of the remaining nominal capital.
3	C	S 874 states that the charge is void, not voidable (Option B), if not registered within 21 days of creation; the existence of subsequent secured creditors is irrelevant (Option D). The charge however is the security for the debt, not the debt itself which remains valid; thus it is not inevitable that the creditor will receive nothing (Option A).
4	C	S 245 Insolvency Act 1986 states that a floating charge is invalid if created within 12 months of the onset of insolvency if it secures an existing debt.

5	C	A listed plc may hold up to 10% of its shares in 'treasury' to sell on in future without the usual formalities.
6	A	Distributable profits are accumulated realised profits less accumulated realised losses.
7	C	Where shareholders had reasonable grounds to believe the distribution contravened the Act, the excess amount is repayable.
8	C	A company's constitution includes its articles, resolutions and agreements. A prospectus may include details of the rights attaching to a particular class of share but it is not a constitutional source.
9	C	The cancellation of calls is one of the three scenarios envisaged in s 641 for the reduction of capital.
10	B	A solvency statement must be made for the coming year.

37 Ethics and business 1

1	B	Objectivity requires intellectual honesty and keeping your mind free from bias. A and D both describe integrity and option C describes professional competence.
2	A	Requests by a regulator usually require an accountant to disclose confidential information. Requests by a fellow employee, an employer or a client may allow disclosure but the accountant is not obliged to disclose them if they do not wish to. Lawyers cannot oblige an accountant to disclose information.
3	D	An important principle of professional competence is not taking on work if you are not competent to do it.

4
	By keeping their mind free from distractions.
✓	By seeking supporting evidence before accepting information is accurate.
✓	By investigating why information was given to them.
✓	By reviewing the work of a junior before accepting it as correct.
	By being straightforward and honest at all times.

The correct options demonstrate questioning and non-acceptance that work is correct on face value.

5	B	Accountability can be demonstrated by taking responsibility for your own actions.
6	D	Financial information is publicly available and citizens use it as a basis to invest their money. Therefore accountants have a social responsibility to ensure it is as accurate as possible.

7
	Financial responsibility
✓	Respect
✓	Social responsibility
✓	Courtesy
	Confidence

Financial responsibility and confidence are not explicitly mentioned by the code.

8	A	Both codes are essentially the same but CIMA's has some adjustments to ensure it fits with local regulations.
9		Selflessness, honesty, openness, leadership.
10	B	This is the most correct option. The APB and POB are sub-bodies of the FRC. In Options C and D, both bodies carry out other important work, not just the ones given.

38 Ethics and business 2

1
- ☑ To prevent passing on misinformation.
- ☐ To prevent bias affecting an accountant's work.
- ☑ To enhance the credibility of an accountant's work.
- ☐ To protect the security of information.
- ☑ To ensure straightforward and honest dealings.

By applying integrity, accountants seek to minimise the risk of passing on incorrect information and this enhances the credibility of their work. Straightforwardness and honesty are also important.

2	C	Companies should develop policies and practices to ensure they play a full part in the local community.
3	A	The other qualities are respect, reliability and responsibility.
4	C	IFAC's mission is to enhance the quality of services and to develop high professional standards of accountants.
5	B	Enforcement is not an essential element, it may actually be counter-productive.
6		Responsibility, professional, accountability, scepticism.
7	B	The Seven Principles of Public Life do not make such a requirement.
8	A	IFAC's code, like CIMA's, is based on ethical principles rather than compliance.
9	D	The code can be used as a basis for judging a member's behaviour against what is expected of them. It does not include legal obligations, is not evidence that all members meet IFAC's criteria and is not required due to CIMA's chartered status.
10	C	The statement describes integrity.

39 Ethics and business 3

1	C	There is no legal obligation to follow the code.
2	B	The accountant maintains their 'independence of appearance'.
3	B	Setting personal and career goals would not help a CIMA member act in the public interest or in a socially responsible manner.
4	D	Accountants are accountable for their own judgements and decisions.

5   A   Codes of practice seek to enhance the standards of behaviour of members. They cannot eliminate unethical behaviour entirely, but it indicates a minimum level of behaviour expected. Codes can be rules-based, not just principles-based.

6

Phrase	Compliance-based	Ethics-based
Law based	✓	
Detection	✓	
Principles based		✓
Discretionary		✓

Compliance-based approaches advocate enforcing the law and detection processes. Ethics-based approaches use principles and are discretionary in application.

7   C   Part C contains this guidance.

8   ☑ Professional behaviour

         ☐ Leadership

         ☑ Confidentiality

         ☑ Professional competence

         ☐ Openness

         Leadership and openness are included in the Seven Principles of Public Life.

9   C   The other options describe the rules-based approach to developing a code.

10   D   Review is not part of CIMA's Professional Development Cycle.

40 Ethical conflict 1

1   C   Professional behaviour. Their actions are certainly dishonest and may constitute fraud.

2   A   Objectivity. It could appear to a reasonable observer that you received the holiday in return for accepting the loan.

3   B   Professional competence and due care. The colleague is unlikely to be able to exercise due care if they have consumed a bottle of wine.

4   D   Confidentiality. The database contains personal information about the members that should only be used by your employer. Supplying the information to a third party (your father) breaches that confidentiality.

5   B   Integrity. The continued use of estimates risks inaccurate trade receivables and payables and therefore misleading accounts.

6   C   A CIMA member should always look to resolve the matter themselves before taking it further.

7   Societal, professional, personal, corporate.

8   A   Professional competence means only taking on work that you are suitably qualified to do.

9

- [✓] Professional bodies may lose their 'chartered' status.
- [✓] Increased regulation of the profession by external organisations.
- [ ] Increased employability of accountants.
- [ ] Improved reputation of the profession.
- [✓] Reduced public trust in the profession.

Professional bodies can lose their 'chartered' status if they are no longer seen to act in the public interest. The profession may be subject to external regulation or legal regulation by government if it cannot regulate itself adequately. The public will lose trust in it.

10   B   Legal advice should always be taken before breaching any duty of confidentiality to minimise any risk of legal action by the affected party. A and D both involve breaching confidentiality, and C would mean the accountant behaving unethically and at risk of disciplinary action by CIMA.

41 Ethical conflict 2

1   C   The law always overrides professional and personal ethics.

2

Statement	True	False
Unethical behaviour will always be punished with a criminal conviction		✓
CIMA students are expected to demonstrate the same level of professional standards as full members.	✓	
A conflict of interest is evidence of wrongdoing.		✓
Societal values are encompassed in the law.	✓	

Unethical behaviour is not always criminal behaviour. A conflict of interest describes a situation where an individual has competing professional or personal interests. It is virtually impossible for finance professionals to avoid conflicts entirely. It only becomes wrongdoing if the professional exploits the situation for his or her own benefit.

3   B   Supply of such information is insider-dealing – a criminal offence.

4   B   The CIMA code provides that where the resolution of an ethical dilemma requires breach of confidence, the member should seek legal advice or consult CIMA.

5   A   Providing misleading information breaches the fundamental principle of integrity.

6

- [✓] Working part-time for two rival businesses.
- [ ] Owning shares in a company that competes with your employer.
- [✓] Being employed by a close relative.
- [✓] Being offered a valuable gift by a friend who is also a business contact.
- [ ] Receiving a performance bonus from your manager.

Owning shares in a company that competes with your employer does not create a conflict of interest, as you are not in a position to affect its results. The performance bonus would only cause a conflict if you were able to determine if you were eligible.

7	D	Although ethical accountants may in some cases help improve the profitability of companies, they cannot 'ensure' companies are profitable. Interfering with a company's results to make them profitable is unethical behaviour.

8

- [✓] Meetings that take place.
- [✓] Decisions that are taken.
- [✓] Informal discussions and phone calls.
- [ ] Their day-to-day feelings.
- [ ] Advice from their families.

The accountant should keep a record of all professional and business communications, meetings and decisions as they may be important evidence that the member has done all they can to resolve the issue.

9	D	Whilst you might find it easier to talk to a close colleague, this approach could lead to a breach of confidentiality. You should consult with your line manager first, unless they are part of the problem. The Audit Committee or even the board of directors could be contacted in the event of major problems. CIMA is always available for consultation.
10	C	You should avoid activities that threaten your professional standards.

42 Ethical conflict 3

1

- [ ] To reply to a solicitor who is representing a past employee who is suing your employer.
- [ ] To enable the accurate preparation of a report for a departmental manager.
- [✓] When the person the information concerns has given you permission.
- [✓] To defend yourself in a claim for misconduct.
- [✓] When you are obliged legally.

All these circumstances would permit you to disclose the information. A letter from a solicitor does not legally oblige you to disclose the information, nor does the preparation of a report.

2	B	'I did not know' is no excuse if the accountant should have been reasonably aware of the problem, even if not made aware of it explicitly.
3	A	Ethical dilemmas involve unclear choices about what is right and wrong. Accountants should trust their instincts and seek advice where appropriate.

4

- [✓] Taking on work from a company that is in direct competition with their employer
- [✓] When the income from one private client exceeds the salary received from their main employer
- [ ] A private client asks the accountant to work for them full-time
- [ ] Having to turn down private work as they do not have sufficient spare time to do the work
- [✓] When the accountant needs to leave their employer's office to deal with an emergency with a private client.

Working for direct competitors will create a conflict as each would require the accountant to put their interests first. High fee income from one private client may cause the accountant to put their needs before those of their employer. A job offer is not a conflict of interest. Turning down work is an example of preventing a conflict of interest as the accountant is only taking on work they can do in the time they have available – no party is disadvantaged. Emergencies involving private clients may cause a conflict if the accountant needs to decide whether or not to stay in their employer's office or go to see the client.

5   B   Integrity is about accuracy; this is most likely to be at risk when rushing to meet a deadline as mistakes are more likely.

6   D   Professional competence and due care is about being competent to do a job and paying close attention to what you are doing. When attempting to do something for the first time the most relevant principle you are likely to breach is the principle of competence.

7   D   Career aspirations are not relevant to making an ethical decision. The right decision should be taken regardless of the impact it might have. This is why some ethical decisions are difficult to take.

8   Relevant, principles, ethical, internal.

9   B   Gifts and hospitality may be seen by others as reward for 'special favours' and may bias future work.

10   A   The manager represents corporate values, accounting standards represent professional values.

43 Corporate governance 1

1   C   The forum has 15 members.

2   A   Enron hid massive borrowing debts by using off-balance sheet financing techniques.

3

- [✓] Active management by Fund Managers
- [ ] Stock market crashes in the 1990's
- [✓] Loss of confidence in financial statements and company management
- [✓] A number of high profile scandals and corporate collapses
- [ ] A poor standard of company legislation.

Stock market crashes had no bearing on the need to develop corporate governance rules. Company legislation was not considered poor.

4

Statement	True	False
Business efficacy	✓	
Fiduciary duties of directors		✓
Accountability	✓	
Profitability		✓

Corporate governance is concerned with effective controls, business efficacy and accountability – not fiduciary duties or profitability.

5   C   The form of payment should not adversely affect a company provided the bonus scheme is correctly set up. By increasing their company's share price, the directors should have improved the financial position of the company, which is to the company's benefit.

6   A   The Combined Code has not affected the fundamental duty of skill and care of executive directors.

7   A   Employees are a financial stakeholder.

8   B   The management board is comprised entirely of managers and is concerned with the day-to-day running of the business. It is monitored by the supervisory board consisting of members elected by the shareholders to safeguard stakeholder interests.

9   D   The code states that remuneration committees should have at least three independent non-executive directors on board.

10   (a)(ii), (b)(iii), (c)(i). Turnbull reported on internal controls, Higgs on non-executive directors and Smith on audit committees.

44 Corporate governance 2

1   A   The answer is the definition from the Cadbury Committee. Remember that governance is about how companies are run, not how directors are regulated.

2   B   The Public Company Accounting Oversight Board was created by Sarbanes-Oxley.

3   D   The Cadbury Committee recommended that service contracts for directors should not exceed three years.

4   B   The European Commission developed a series of directives on corporate governance for member states to follow.

5   A   All non-executive boards are not practical, as the board needs input from those running the day-to-day operations.

6
☐	The qualifications of employees
☑	The risk and control systems
☑	The communication of its strategies through the organisation
☑	The human capital within the business
☐	The bank account balance

The qualifications of employees and bank account balances are items which may be monitored but this role is likely to be delegated by the board.

7

Statement	True	False
Listed companies must state in their accounts that they complied or did not comply with the Combined Code.	✓	
Non-compliance with the code creates a civil liability that the directors may be sued for.		✓
Non-compliance with the code may result in the directors being liable for wrongful trading.		✓
Directors of non-compliant companies may be disqualified from acting as a director for up to five years.		✓

Non-compliance is not a criminal or civil offence and will not result in disqualification of directors. Listed companies must state in their accounts whether or not they complied with the Code.

8   D   This is the role of the supervisory board.

9   A   Directors should review internal controls annually and report to the shareholders that they have done so.

10   C   The Combined Code is the main source of corporate governance rules in the UK. Sarbanes-Oxley is the source of US regulations and the Cadbury Report is included as a part of the Combined Code.

45 Corporate governance 3

1
- ✓ Internal controls to protect a company's assets
- ✓ The board of directors providing employees with a mission statement
- ☐ Stock exchange rules that dictate when shareholders may buy and sell shares
- ✓ An employee performance related pay scheme
- ☐ CIMA's Fundamental Principles

Stock Exchange rules are external rules that apply to the shareholders of a company, and do not affect how the company is run. CIMA's Fundamental Principles apply to CIMA members not businesses.

2
- ✓ Shareholders
- ☐ Regulators
- ✓ Suppliers
- ☐ Competitors
- ✓ The Government

Regulators and competitors are interest shareholders.

3   A   Most companies in the UK and USA operate unitary boards. French companies may use a unitary board, or a two-tier board like Germany.

4	C	Splitting the chairman and chief executive role is recommended under corporate governance guidance. Companies are legally required to provide health and safety training and not to discriminate against candidates because of the age, sex, religion or any disabilities.
5	C	Shareholders do not need corporate governance rules to be able to sue directors. There is no serious mistrust of financial statements by stock markets. Corporate governance rules were developed to help protect stakeholders from corporate collapses, to improve financial reporting and to facilitate the globalisation of investment, not to ensure all companies act ethically.
6	B	Shareholder activism relates to the level of involvement a company's shareholders have in running the organisation.
7	D	The audit committee should include at least 3 independent non-executive directors.
8	C	Regular shareholder contact is good corporate governance.
9	B	The London Stock Exchange requires all companies listed on the exchange to comply with the Combined Code.
10	C	Social responsibility policies must reflect the organisation's values.

Mock assessments

CIMA

Paper C5 (Certificate)

Fundamentals of Ethics, Corporate Governance and Business Law

Mock Assessment 1

Question Paper	
Time allowed	**2 hours**
Answer ALL the questions	

DO NOT OPEN THIS PAPER UNTIL YOU ARE READY TO START UNDER EXAMINATION CONDITIONS

Answer ALL questions

1   Exe Ltd was under contract to deliver goods by road to London for Wye Ltd for £2,000. After part of the journey was completed, the delivery vehicle broke down and Wye Ltd was forced to arrange for Zed Ltd to complete the delivery.

If there are no provisions in the contract to deal with this situation, which of the following is **correct**?

A   Exe Ltd is entitled to part of the delivery fee
B   Exe Ltd is entitled to nothing
C   Exe Ltd is entitled to a reasonable sum for the work done
D   Exe Ltd is entitled to the full £2,000

2   Which **three** of the following must be included on a statement of written particulars of employment?

☐ Names of employer and employee
☐ Date on which employment began
☐ Pay rate and intervals at which it is paid
☐ Set holiday dates in the first year of employment
☐ Details of disciplinary methods

3   Which of the following minority rights is **not** correct?

A   Right to apply to the court in respect of unfairly prejudicial conduct
B   Right to petition the Government for winding up on the just and equitable ground
C   Right of 15% of members of a class to apply to the court for cancellation of a variation of their rights
D   Right of 200+ members to apply to the Government to investigate the company's affairs

4   Which of the following are **correct** differences between Sharia and Codified law systems?

(i)   Sharia law transcends national boundaries
(ii)   Judges under Sharia law cannot create law
(iii) Codified law is written by man
(iv)   There is no codification of laws under Sharia law

A   (i), (ii) and (iii) only
B   (i) and (iii) only
C   (ii), (iii) and (iv) only
D   All of the above

5   Which of the following remedies is **not** available for a breach of a contract to provide personal services?

A   Damages
B   A decree of specific performance
C   An injunction
D   An action for the price

6   What is corporate governance?

    A   Stock market regulations which govern how public companies are run

    B   Ethical guidelines for directors

    C   The system by which companies are directed and controlled

    D   Directors' legal obligations

7   Which of the following is an example of how company law has influenced a company's corporate governance?

    A   A public company that splits the role of chairman and chief executive

    B   A public company that sets up an audit committee

    C   A public company that sets directors' notice periods at one year or less

    D   A public company that has an annual general meeting

8   Which **three** of the following may require Parliamentary input to give effect to them?

    ☐   Delegated legislation

    ☐   Statute

    ☐   EU regulations

    ☐   EU directives

    ☐   EU decisions

9   In which of the following is there a presumption that legal relations are intended?

    A   A promise by a father to make a gift to his son

    B   A commercial transaction

    C   A domestic arrangement

    D   A social arrangement

10   Which of the following statements about issuing shares is **not** correct?

    A   Directors of private companies with one class of share have authority to issue shares unless this is restricted by the articles

    B   Only directors of public companies must seek approval from the members before allotting shares

    C   Authority given to directors to allot shares must state the maximum number of shares that can be allotted

    D   If authority is not granted by the articles, an ordinary resolution is required to give directors authority to allot shares

11   Which of the following describes the minimum requirement for members to requisition a general meeting of a public company?

    A   Members holding not less than 5% of the company's issued share capital which carries voting rights

    B   Members holding not less than 10% of the company's issued share capital which carries voting rights

    C   Members holding not less than 20% of the company's issued share capital which carries voting rights

    D   Members holding not less than 50% of the company's issued share capital which carries voting rights

12 Which **three** of the following statements describe the activities regulated by the Professional Oversight Board?

☐ Registration of members of accountancy bodies

☐ Training and education of members of accountancy bodies

☐ Development of accounting regulations on behalf of accountancy bodies

☐ Application of accounting regulations by members of accountancy bodies

☐ Conduct and discipline of members of accountancy bodies

13 ABC Ltd has contracted with DEF Ltd. If ABC Ltd acts in breach of a warranty, which of the following is/are **correct**?

(i)   DEF Ltd may terminate the contract and sue for damages

(ii)   DEF Ltd may sue for damages but may not terminate the contract

(iii) DEF Ltd may ignore the breach and continue with the contract

A   (i) only

B   (i) and (iii) only

C   (ii) and (iii) only

D   All of the above

14 Which of the following is **not** a board committee suggested by the Combined Code?

A   Audit

B   Investment

C   Nomination

D   Remuneration

15 Which of the following statements is **correct**?

A   All English courts must apply European Law even if it contradicts English Law.

B   If European and English Law conflict, English courts cannot apply either law.

C   An English court must apply English Law unless it obtains the Government's permission to apply European Law.

D   All English courts are obliged to apply English Law even if it contradicts European Law.

16 When obtaining professional advice to resolve an ethical conflict, special care must be taken to avoid breaching which fundamental ethical principle?

A   Integrity

B   Objectivity

C   Confidentiality

D   Professional behaviour

17 The maximum total period of statutory maternity leave that a woman may be entitled to is:

A   Six weeks

B   Twelve weeks

C   Twenty-six weeks

D   Fifty-two weeks

18   Which **three** of the following describe how an accountant can develop their personal quality of respect?

☐ By developing constructive relationships with others

☐ By recognising the rights of others

☐ By avoiding disagreements with others

☐ By not challenging the views of those more qualified than them

☐ By arguing their own opinion but accepting the views of others

---

19   In the event of an accountant's professional ethics being in conflict with a contractual obligation, what course of action should be taken?

A   The accountant should meet their contractual obligation at the expense of their professional ethics

B   The accountant should follow their professional ethics at the expense of their contractual obligation

C   The accountant should act in accordance with their personal ethics

D   The accountant should follow any advice given to them by their employer

---

20   Which of the following is an example of how business ethics may influence corporate governance?

A   When a business chooses a supplier on the basis of cost

B   When a business chooses a supplier on the basis of product quality

C   When a business chooses a supplier on the basis of its employees' working conditions

D   When a business chooses a supplier on the basis of speed of delivery

---

21   Which of the following would strongly indicate that a person was an employee?

A   He uses his own tools

B   He is delegated work

C   He renders invoices to the company

D   He has a contract with the company

---

22   The repeated practice of certain principles can create an obligation to continue to do so in the future. This is a source of law under which system?

A   Common law

B   Codified systems

C   Sharia law

D   International law

---

23   Which **three** of the following statements concerning company meetings are **correct**?

☐ Members holding 10% of the voting rights of a private company may requisition a meeting, this is reduced to 5% if the company has not held a meeting for 12 months

☐ Members holding a minimum of 95% of the voting rights of a private company must agree if the notice period for a general meeting is to be waived

☐ A poll can be demanded by members or proxies representing at least 10% of the voting rights

☐ Results of a quoted company poll must be published on its website

☐ Proxies are not included in the calculation when deciding whether or not a quorum exists

24 You are working as an assistant management accountant in a large manufacturing company and your role involves costing new products. A long-time supplier has invited you and your colleagues out for lunch.

Do you have an ethical dilemma?

A No dilemma
B Yes, a risk of breaking integrity
C Yes, a risk of breaking objectivity
D Yes, a risk of breaking confidentiality

25 Your manager has passed you their work for you to double-check. You find a large number of errors but your manager insists it is fine and tells you to send it to the finance director.

Do you have an ethical dilemma?

A No dilemma
B Yes, a risk of breaking objectivity
C Yes, a risk of breaking integrity
D Yes, a risk of breaking confidentiality

26 Whilst working in your company's payroll department, an employee has asked you to post their salary details to a building society in support their mortgage application. You have been given the name and address of the person dealing with the application at the building society and the approval from the payroll manager to send out the details.

Do you have an ethical dilemma?

A No dilemma
B Yes, a risk of breaking professional competence
C Yes, a risk of breaking confidentiality
D Yes, a risk of breaking objectivity

27 A colleague has recently gained promotion and you have taken over their work on the receivables ledger. During the hand-over, the colleague gives you a list of customers that he calls 'trouble-makers'. He says, 'you won't get on with them, they are all rude and never pay on time'.

Do you have an ethical dilemma?

A No dilemma
B Yes, a risk of breaking professional behaviour
C Yes, a risk of breaking confidentiality
D Yes, a risk of breaking objectivity

28 On a Friday night out in town you meet with a friend who works for a company that supplies materials to yours. Your friend's employer is facing closure, but earlier that day you learned that your company awarded them a new contract that will save it. The supplier will announce the news to its employees first thing on Monday morning, but your friend is obviously still very concerned that their job may be at risk. They know that their company tendered for the contract and they ask if you have heard anything.

Do you have an ethical dilemma?

A   No dilemma

B   Yes, a risk of breaking confidentiality

C   Yes, a risk of breaking due care

D   Yes, a risk of breaking objectivity

---

29   Tee Ltd placed some computers in its shop window with a notice which read:

'Special offer, Internet-ready computers for sale at £400'

Which of the following is/are **correct**?

(i)   The notice amounts to an invitation to treat

(ii)   When Anne called in to the shop and offered £350 for one of the computers, she had made a counter offer

(iii)   Tee Ltd is obliged to sell a computer to anyone who can pay the price

A   (i) and (ii) only

B   (i) only

C   (ii) only

D   All of the above

---

30   Charles recently purchased some goods at an auction sale

Which of the following is/are **correct**?

(i)   The contract was concluded by the fall of the auctioneer's hammer

(ii)   The auctioneer's call for bids was an invitation to treat

A   (i) only

B   (ii) only

C   Both (i) and (ii)

D   Neither (i) nor (ii)

---

31   An employer must provide an employee with a written statement of particulars of the employment

A   Within one month of the employment commencing

B   As soon after the commencement of employment as possible

C   Within two months of the employment commencing

D   Within a reasonable time of the employment commencing

---

32   Which **three** of the following are documents that must be sent to the Registrar when registering a company?

☐   Certificate of incorporation

☐   Articles of association

☐   Memorandum of association

☐   Statement of compliance

☐   Statement of proposed officers

33 Which of the following documents is submitted to the Registrar when registering a new company and contains the details of the intended address of the registered office?

A The articles of association
B The statement of proposed officers
C The application for registration
D The statement of compliance

34 Which of the following is **not** contained in a company's certificate of incorporation?

A The company's date of incorporation

B The company's registered number

C Whether the company is quoted or not quoted

D Whether the company's registered office is in England and Wales, Wales, Scotland or Northern Ireland

35 What resolution(s) can be used by a private company to alter its articles of association?
(i) Special
(ii) Ordinary
(iii) Written

A (i) only
B (i) and (iii)
C (i) and (ii)
D (ii) and (iii)

36 Which of the following statements is **incorrect**?

A Payment by the debtor of less than the full amount of the debt will satisfy the whole debt at common law, if paid early at the request of the creditor.

B Payment by a third party of less than the full amount of the debt will discharge the whole debt at common law, if agreed by the creditor.

C Payment by the debtor of less than the full amount of the debt will discharge the whole debt at common law, if agreed to by the creditor.

D Payment of less than the full amount of the debt will discharge the whole debt at common law, if extra consideration is provided by the debtor.

37 Consider the following statements concerning how judges deal with cases.

(i) Under common law, the judge will consider the facts, relevant statute law and all previous similar cases.

(ii) Under codified systems, judges may only consider the facts and apply the letter of the law.

(iii) Under Sharia law, a judge will apply the law to the facts presented, turning to the Sunnah for guidance on interpretation if necessary.

Which statements is/are **correct**?

- **A** (i) and (ii)
- **B** (i) and (iii)
- **C** (ii) and (iii)
- **D** (iii) only

---

38 An employee should ensure the health and safety at work of whom?

- **A** Employees
- **B** Independent contractors
- **C** Visitors
- **D** All of the above

---

39 Which of the following, according to CIMA, is a fundamental principle that must be observed by all members?

- **A** Honesty
- **B** Accountability
- **C** Confidentiality
- **D** Leadership

---

40 Which **three** of the following indicate poor corporate governance?

- ☐ Domination of the board by a single individual
- ☐ Board focus on short-term profitability
- ☐ The payment of bonuses to directors
- ☐ Contradictory information given to stakeholders
- ☐ An employee discovering errors in a report after following company checking procedures

---

41 Which of the following statements are **correct**?

- (i) A public company cannot commence trading until it has received a certificate from the Registrar confirming that it has satisfied the requirement regarding allotted share capital
- (ii) Under s 122 of the Insolvency Act 1986 a court may wind up a public company that does not obtain a trading certificate within one year of incorporation
- (iii) A private company may commence trading upon receipt of its certificate of incorporation

- **A** (i) and (ii) only
- **B** (ii) and (iii) only
- **C** (i) and (iii) only
- **D** All of the above

---

42 Which of the following is a characteristic of the ethics-based approach to a code of ethics?

- **A** Explicit
- **B** Judgement
- **C** Detection
- **D** Rules

---

43 Which of the following statements is/are **incorrect**?

(i) Legal title cannot pass on a contract induced by misrepresentation
(ii) Misrepresentation renders a contract voidable
(iii) A victim of negligent misrepresentation may seek rescission and damages

A (i) only
B (ii) only
C (i) and (iii)
D (ii) and (iii)

44 The legal system of which country uses mediation committees to hear the vast majority of cases?

A Malaysia
B China
C Sri Lanka
D Greece

45 In the civil court system of the UK, in which court do cases for small sums of money generally start?

A The Crown Court
B The Chancery Division of the High Court
C The County Court
D The Magistrates' Court

46 Which of the following is categorised as a financial stakeholder in a company?

A The media
B Activist groups
C Competitors
D The Government

47 Which three of the following courts are bound by a decision of the High Court ?

☐ Magistrates' Court
☐ County Court
☐ Crown Court
☐ Privy Council
☐ Court of Appeal

48 According to CIMA's guidance for resolving ethical dilemmas, what should a CIMA member do once they have considered the alternative courses of action (and their consequences) open to them?

A Select a course of action consistent with fundamental principles
B Consult with appropriate persons within their organisation
C Obtain professional or legal advice
D Change roles or departments

49 Which of the following is **not** correct?

A An employer is obliged to provide an employee with a reference

B An employer must allow trade union officials reasonable paid time off work to perform their trade union duties

C An employer must provide an employee with a safe working environment

D Employees with less than one month's service are not entitled to receive statutory notice if dismissed

50 Which of the following statements is/are **correct**?

(i) If an agreement is stated to be 'binding in honour only', the parties have decided that the agreement should not have contractual force

(ii) If an agreement is not in writing, the parties are presumed to have intended that it should not be legally enforceable

A (i) only
B (ii) only
C Neither (i) nor (ii)
D Both (i) and (ii)

51 Which of the following statements describes treasury shares?

A Shares issued by a public company to a creditor
B A public company's own shares that it legitimately purchased out of distributable profit
C Shares held by a public company as an investment
D Shares that can be repurchased from shareholders at a later date by the issuing company

52 A company has issued and allotted 100 £1 shares. On application it received 30p per share and has recently collected a further 60p per share. What is the value of its called up share capital?

A £30
B £60
C £90
D £100

53 Which method of selling shares to the public by a public company is described below.

'An invitation to the public to apply for shares in a company based on information contained in a prospectus'

A A public offer
B A placing
C An allotment
D An offer for sale

54 Interest payments to debentureholders must be paid out of:

A Distributable profit
B Pre-tax profit
C The capital redemption reserve
D The share premium account

55 On 1 August 20X7 Jan created a fixed charge for £50,000 over the assets of Blox Ltd and it was registered on 1 October 20X7. On 1 September 20X7 a fixed charge for £100,000 was created (over the same assets) on behalf of Ade. Ade's fixed charge was registered on 15 September 20X7.

Which of the following statements describes the priority of the two fixed charges?

A   Jan's fixed charge has priority as it was created first
B   Ade's fixed charge has priority as it was registered within 21 days of creation
C   Both charges rank equally in priority as they are both fixed
D   Ade's fixed charge has priority as it has a greater value

---

56 Which of the following event(s) cause the crystallisation of a floating charge?

(i)   The liquidation of the company
(ii)   The appointment of a receiver by the chargee
(iii)   The sale of an asset subject to a fixed charge even if the floating charge is not secured on it
(iv)   The cessation of the company's business

A   (i) only
B   (ii) only
C   (i), (ii) and (iv) only
D   All of the above

---

57 Which of the following statements is/are **correct**?

(i)   An employer has an implied duty to behave reasonably and responsibly towards employees.
(ii)   An employer has an implied duty to provide facilities for smokers

A   (i) only
B   (ii) only
C   Neither (i) nor (ii)
D   Both (i) and (ii)

---

58 Who suggested that ethical behaviour can be developed by individuals who have a strong foundation of fundamental virtues such as honesty, integrity and openness?

A   Kant
B   Plato
C   Aristotle
D   Confucius

---

59 An accountant who recognises that when their judgements and decisions are called into question they are ultimately responsible, is demonstrating which professional quality?

A   Independence
B   Accountability
C   Social responsibility
D   Scepticism

---

60 Other than contracts by deed, how long does a claimant have to bring an action for breach of contract before they are statute-barred?

A One year
B Two years
C Six years
D Eight years

61 Which of CIMA's fundamental principles is described below?

'Accountants should act fairly and not allow prejudice, bias, or the influence of others to affect their judgements'.

A Integrity
B Confidentiality
C Professional competence
D Objectivity

62 Which of the following decisions would a board of directors **not** become involved in?

A The purchase of a new computer network
B The disposal of one company car
C The choice of bank loan to support the purchase of a new factory
D The size of the advertising budget

63 Which **three** of the following are characteristics of limited companies?

☐ Perpetual succession
☐ Limited liability of the business organisation
☐ Shares may not be sold publicly
☐ Separate legal entity
☐ Limited liability of members

64 Which of the following principles of public life is described below?

'Individuals should act solely in the public interest and not for personal gain or that of friends and family'.

A Integrity
B Honesty
C Openness
D Selflessness

65 Which of the following statements is **correct**?

A If a person signs a contract, he/she is bound by all its terms
B A contract which has not been signed is not binding on any of the parties
C A person who signs a contract is deemed to have read it
D A person who has not read a contract cannot be bound by it

66 In respect of misrepresentation, which of the following are **correct**?

Select all that apply.

☐ The person entering the contract must have been aware of the statement's existence

☐ The statement can have been made to the public at large

☐ It is sufficient that the misrepresentor knows that the statement will be passed on to the other party

☐ Silence is not generally misrepresentation

☐ What has been said must be complete enough not to mislead

67 The articles of association of Dee Ltd, a property development company, states that the company has power to borrow when purchasing land and that the directors have authority to borrow up to £200,000. The board has resolved to purchase a piece of land for £300,000. The Midwest Bank plc has agreed to make a loan of £250,000 to Dee Ltd to acquire the land.

Which of the following is **correct**?

A The loan is void as Dee Ltd has acted *ultra vires*

B As the directors have exceeded their authority, the bank cannot enforce the loan against Dee Ltd

C As the directors have resolved to obtain the loan, the transaction is lawful

D The loan is *ultra vires* the directors but is valid as far as Midwest Bank plc is concerned

68 Which body oversees the accountancy profession globally?

A CIMA

B The Professional Oversight Board for Accountancy

C The Financial Reporting Council

D IFAC

69 What is the maximum recommended length for director service contracts according to the Combined Code?

A One year

B Two years

C Three years

D Five years

70 Which of the following statements about consumer contracts is/are **correct**?

(i) A contractual term which attempts to exclude liability for damage to property caused by negligence is void unless reasonable

(ii) A contractual term which attempts to exclude liability for death or personal injury is void

A (i) only

B (ii) only

C Neither (i) nor (ii)

D Both (i) and (ii)

71   In which country's legal system would you find the *Sejm* and the *Senate*?

    A   Poland
    B   Italy
    C   Cyprus
    D   Denmark

72   Which of the following statements is/are **correct**?

    (i)   A contract of employment must be in writing
    (ii)   An employer must provide written particulars of the employment for the employee

    A   (i) only
    B   (ii) only
    C   Both (i) and (ii)
    D   Neither (i) nor (ii)

73   Which of CIMA's fundamental principles is described below?

    'Accountants should be straightforward and honest in all professional and business relationships'.

    A   Objectivity
    B   Confidentiality
    C   Due care
    D   Integrity

74   What best practice does the Combined Code recommend regarding the roles of chairman and chief executive?

    A   The chairman must previously have been the chief executive
    B   The chairman and chief executive roles should ideally not be performed by one individual
    C   The chairman should not have previously been chief executive
    D   The chairman and chief executive roles should be combined if possible

75   A Ltd placed the following advertisement in a local newspaper:

    'We are able to offer for sale a number of portable colour television sets at the specially reduced price of £5.90. Order now while stocks last.'

    The advertisement contained a mistake in that the television sets should have been priced at £59.00. B Ltd immediately placed an order for 100 television sets.

    Which of the following statements is **correct**?

    A   B Ltd has accepted an offer and is contractually entitled to the 100 television sets.
    B   A Ltd can refuse to supply B Ltd as the advertisement is not an offer, but an invitation to treat.
    C   A Ltd can only refuse to sell the television sets to B Ltd if it has sold all its stock.
    D   As B Ltd has not yet paid for the television sets, the company has no contractual right to them.

Mock assessment 1
Answers

**DO NOT TURN THIS PAGE UNTIL YOU HAVE
COMPLETED THE MOCK ASSESSMENT 1**

| 1 | B | Exe Ltd is entitled to nothing as the contract has not been completely performed. |

2

- ☑ Names of employer and employee
- ☑ Date on which employment began
- ☑ Pay rate and intervals at which it is paid
- ☐ Set holiday dates in the first year of employment
- ☐ Details of disciplinary methods

3	B	The right to petition for winding up is a right to petition **the court**, not the Government.
4	A	Sharia law is based on the religion of Islam and it transcends national boundaries, whereas countries adopting a codified system have laws specific to them. Muslims believe that the Quran is directly sourced from God (Allah) whereas codified law is man made. Judges in Sharia systems cannot create law. There is some codification of Sharia law where some Sharia practices have developed through customs.
5	B	Specific performance will never be granted in a contract for personal services.
6	C	Corporate governance is the system by which organisations are directed and controlled.
7	D	Under the Companies Act 2006 public companies must have an AGM. The other options are recommendations of the Combined Code which is not company law.

8

- ☑ Delegated legislation
- ☑ Statute
- ☐ EU regulations
- ☑ EU directives
- ☐ EU decisions

Most delegated legislation must be laid before Parliament and therefore some Parliamentary input may be involved before it has effect. Parliament is involved at all stages of producing statute law.

EU regulations have direct effect and therefore have the force of law in member states without the need for legislation to be passed by them. EU Directives do not have direct effect and member states must pass legislation to give them the force of law. EU decisions are immediately binding on the recipient without the need for Parliamentary input.

9	B	*Rose and Frank v Crompton:* legal relations are presumed in commercial transactions.
10	B	Directors of private companies with more than one class of share as well as directors of public companies must seek approval of the members before they can allot shares. The authority given to directors must state the maximum number of shares that can be allotted and requires an ordinary resolution to pass it.
11	B	Members holding not less than 10% of the company's issued share capital which carries voting rights can requisition a general meeting. The figure is 5% for private companies that have not held a general meeting for 12 months.

12   ☑ Registration of members of accountancy bodies

☑ Training and education of members of accountancy bodies

☐ Development of accounting regulations on behalf of accountancy bodies

☐ Application of accounting regulations by members of accountancy bodies

☑ Conduct and discipline of members of accountancy bodies

The Professional Oversight Board regulates specific activities of accountancy bodies regarding their members, including their registration and monitoring, training and education, continuous professional development and conduct and discipline.

13   C   You should know the different effects of warranties and conditions in breach.

14   B   An investment committee was not suggested by the Combined Code.

15   A   European Law is regarded as the supreme source of law in all member states.

16   C   While obtaining professional advice you must respect your employer's right to confidentiality unless you have a legal or professional duty to do otherwise.

17   D   Every woman is entitled to fifty-two weeks maternity leave.

18   ☑ By developing constructive relationships with others

☑ By recognising the rights of others

☐ By avoiding disagreements with others

☐ By not challenging the views of those more qualified than them

☑ By arguing their own opinion but accepting the views of others

Accountants should not avoid disagreements nor should they refuse to challenge the views of those more qualified than them. They should however respect that people have different opinions and should not bring disagreements down to a personal level.

19   B   Professional ethics should be followed even if this means breaking a contractual obligation.

20   C   The other options are commercial reasons.

21   B   D could be a contract for services or a contract of employment, A and C both indicate the person is an independent contractor.

22   D   The statement describes international customary law.

23   ☑ Members holding 10% of the voting rights of a private company may requisition a meeting, this is reduced to 5% if the company has not held a meeting for 12 months

☐ Members holding a minimum of 95% of the voting rights of a company must agree if the 14 day notice period for a meeting is to be waived

☑ A poll can be demanded by members or proxies representing at least 10% of the voting rights

☑ Results of a quoted company poll must be published on its website

☐ Proxies are not included in the calculation when deciding whether or not a quorum exists

Members holding a minimum of 90% of the voting rights can agree to waive the notice period. Proxies are counted when deciding whether or not a quorum exists.

24	A	No dilemma. There is no issue of objectivity since the meal is not valuable, has been offered to others, and appears just to be a general goodwill gesture between a supplier and a long-time customer.
25	C	The main principle being broken is integrity. Sending inaccurate information to the finance director makes you party to misinformation.
26	A	No dilemma. There is no issue of confidentiality as the employee and the HR manager have given their permission to send out the details. There is little risk that the information may get into the wrong person's hands as you have the name and address of the person dealing with the application.
27	D	Objectivity. There is a risk that the colleague's statement will prejudice your treatment of the customers in future. You should form your own opinion of them.
28	B	Confidentiality. Even though the friend will find out the good news first thing on Monday, you should still respect confidentiality and not tell them.
29	B	(ii) is incorrect, as such an advertisement would be construed to be invitation to treat, so her statement would be an offer. There is no obligation on Tee Ltd to accept an offer, made by a person in response to the invitation to treat, to buy the computer – so (iii) is incorrect.
30	C	The bids are offers in response to the auctioneer's invitation to treat, and the fall of the hammer accepts the highest offer.
31	C	Unless the employer has already provided a written contract of employment containing the particulars.

32

- ☐ Certificate of incorporation
- ☐ Articles of association
- ☑ Memorandum of association
- ☑ Statement of compliance
- ☑ Statement of proposed officers

The certificate of incorporation is sent by the Registrar once incorporation procedures have been completed. A company does not need to register articles as model articles will be registered by the Registrar if they are not submitted.

33	C	The application for registration contains the details of the intended address of the registered office.
34	C	Other information contained in the certificate of incorporation includes: the company's name, that it is limited by shares or guarantee, and whether it is private or public.
35	B	A private company may alter its articles of association by special resolution or by written resolution with a 75% majority.
36	C	All the other statements are true. If the debtor provides no kind of other consideration for a payment of less than the total, the debt is not discharged.
37	D	Under common law, judges cannot refer to 'all' similar case – the case must have created a precedent. Under codified systems, judges are not limited to the facts and legislation. They are permitted to refer to other previous cases although they are not bound by them.
38	D	An employee is required to take reasonable care at work for the health and safety of themselves and others.

39	C	The other options are part of the seven principles of public life.

40
- ☑ Domination of the board by a single individual
- ☑ Board focus on short-term profitability
- ☐ The payment of bonuses to directors
- ☑ Contradictory information given stakeholders
- ☐ An employee discovering errors in a report after following company checking procedures

The payment of bonuses to directors is mentioned in the Combined Code as a method to improve corporate governance through aligning their remuneration with corporate and individual performance. Errors being discovered after following company procedure is an example of strong corporate governance control procedures, put in place by the directors, that have worked.

41	D	All the statements are correct.
42	B	The other options are characteristics of the compliance approach to a code of ethics.
43	A	It is a general rule of misrepresentation that such a contract is voidable, not void, so legal title can pass.
44	B	The legal system of China involves mediation committees.
45	C	Most small cases start in the County Court.
46	D	The Government is a financial stakeholder, the other options are interest stakeholders.

47
- ☑ Magistrates' Court
- ☑ County Court
- ☑ Crown Court
- ☐ High Court
- ☐ Court of Appeal

The High Court cannot bind a court which is above it in the judicial hierarchy.

48	A	This is the first course of action a CIMA member should take. The other options are valid but at a later stage if the matter is not resolved.
49	A	There is no requirement to provide references.
50	A	A contract may be made orally and no such presumption is made.
51	B	Treasury shares are created when a company buys back its own shares out of distributable profit. Option D describes redeemable shares.
52	C	The called up share capital is the amount the company has required the shareholders to pay on the shares issued. Therefore its called up share capital is ((30p + 60p = 90p) x 100 shares) = £90.
53	D	A public offer is where the public subscribe to the company directly for shares. A placing is a method of raising share capital where there is no public issue of shares. Instead the shares are offered in blocks to persons or institutions who have previously agreed to purchase shares at a predetermined price.

54	B	Debenture interest is paid out of pre-tax profit. Dividends are paid out of distributable profit.
55	B	Usually charges rank in order of creation, but only if they are correctly registered. Jan's charge should have been registered within 21 days of its creation, but this did not happen. Therefore Ade's correctly registered charge has priority even though it was created later.
56	C	The sale of an asset subject to a fixed charge will not cause the crystallisation of a floating charge. The other options will.
57	A	There is no implied duty to provide facilities for smokers. However, the employer must behave reasonably and responsibly towards employees.
58	C	The suggestion has been attributed to the ancient philosopher Aristotle.
59	B	Accountants are accountable for their own judgements and decisions.
60	C	Claimants have six years to bring a claim for breach of contract.
61	D	The statement describes objectivity.
62	B	This is not a major policy or strategic decision.

63

- ☑ Perpetual succession
- ☐ Limited liability of the business organisation
- ☐ Shares may not be sold publicly
- ☑ Separate legal entity
- ☑ Limited liability of members.

A limited company is a legal entity separate from its members and has perpetual succession. Limited liability is that of the members not the company. Shares of public limited companies may be sold publicly. The question did not refer to a private company.

64	D	The statement describes selflessness.
65	C	A is incorrect because if the person signing has been misled about the extent of the terms, they may not be bound.

66

- ☑ The person entering the contract must have been aware of the statement's existence
- ☑ The statement can have been made to the public at large
- ☑ It is sufficient that the misrepresentor knows that the statement would be passed on to the other party
- ☑ Silence is not generally misrepresentation
- ☑ What has been said must be complete enough not to mislead

All the statements are correct.

67	D	Due to s40 Companies Act 2006, the bank cannot be prejudiced due to the *ultra vires* actions of the directors.
68	D	IFAC oversees the accountancy profession globally.
69	A	Services contracts should not exceed one year in length.
70	D	Liability for death or personal injury due to negligence can never be excluded. Exclusion of liability for damage to property is permissible if reasonable in consumer contracts.

71   A   The *Sejm* and the *Senate* are the two houses in Poland's equivalent of the Houses of Parliament.

72   B   An employment contract may be oral, but some written particulars must be provided within 2 months of the employee starting work.

73   D   The statement describes integrity.

74   B   The Code recommends a clear division of power so that one person does not have unfettered powers of decision.

75   B   A newspaper advertisement is an invitation to treat (*Partridge v Crittenden*).

CIMA
Paper C5 (Certificate)
Fundamentals of Ethics, Corporate Governance and Business Law

Mock Assessment 2

Question Paper	
Time allowed	**2 hours**
Answer ALL the questions	

DO NOT OPEN THIS PAPER UNTIL YOU ARE READY TO START UNDER EXAMINATION CONDITIONS

Answer ALL questions

1 Which of the following registers does **not** need to be kept to meet the requirements of the Companies Act 2006?

    A   Register of members
    B   Register of charges
    C   Register or directors' residential addresses
    D   Register of debentureholders

2 Tee Ltd has contracted to use Vee Ltd's 'Grand Hotel' for a business conference. Which of the following would be regarded as a valid reason for the unavailability of the hotel on the agreed date under the law of frustration?

    (i)   The hotel was closed due to flood damage.

    (ii)   The hotel was double booked.

    (iii)   The hotel manager had arranged to have the hotel redecorated. The decorators had failed to complete the work by the agreed date.

    A   (i) only
    B   (iii) only
    C   (ii) and (iii) only
    D   (i), (ii) and (iii)

3 In Sharia law, sayings of the Prophet are known as:

    A   Quran
    B   Figh
    C   Ahadith
    D   Madhab

4 Which part of a case decided by the courts is binding on lower courts dealing with the same material facts?

    A   *Obiter dicta*
    B   The decision of the judge
    C   The *ratio decidendi*
    D   All the above

5 A director of a private company may be removed from office under section 168 of the Companies Act 2006 by:

    A   Ordinary resolution with the usual notice
    B   Written resolution
    C   Ordinary resolution with special notice
    D   Special resolution with special notice

6 Which **three** of the following actions should an accountant follow in order to meet the fundamental principle of professional competence and due care?

☐ An accountant should spend enough time on a job to look into all matters in sufficient detail.

☐ An accountant should refrain from performing services that they cannot perform with reasonable knowledge, competence and diligence

☐ An accountant should only perform work that their employer has deemed them competent at.

☐ An accountant should attend all training and technical update courses available to them even if not relevant to their job.

☐ An accountant should (if relevant) use websites containing technical information to stay up-to-date.

---

7 Which of the following does **not** specifically relate to business ethics?

A The behaviour of employees
B How the business manages its relationships with its stakeholders
C The profitability of the business
D How the business does business

---

8 A Ltd contracted to deliver a quantity of goods to B Ltd for £5,000. The goods were delivered and A Ltd submitted an invoice to B Ltd for the amount due. This contained a number of new terms.

Which of the following is **incorrect**?

A The invoice is a contractual document and B Ltd is bound by the terms on the invoice

B B Ltd is only bound by the terms if it was given notice of them at or before the time of the contract

C B Ltd is bound by the terms if there is a sufficient course of dealings between A Ltd and B Ltd so that B Ltd is assumed to know of the terms

D If B Ltd is unaware of the terms, it can only be bound by them if it agrees to be so

---

9 When deciding upon a course of action to resolve an ethical conflict with an employer, an accountant must make sure the resolution:

A Is acceptable to the employer
B Is consistent with CIMA's fundamental principles
C Ensures the ethical conflict can never happen again
D Has been endorsed by CIMA

---

10 Which **three** of the following have been given the statutory minimum notice period?

☐ Anne, who worked for 10 years and was given 9 weeks' notice

☐ Barry, who worked for 1 week and was summarily dismissed

☐ Catherine, who worked for 5 years and was given two month's notice

☐ David, who has worked for 18 months and was given a week's notice

☐ Emily, who worked for 6 months and was given 3 days' notice

11 Which of the following is **not** a requirement of the Combined Code?

   A   An audit committee should be established

   B   One half of the board should consist of independent non-executive directors

   C   Board members should all attend the AGM

   D   The roles of Chairman and Chief Executive should be combined

12 Which of the following is/are **correct**?

   (i)   A company is owned by its shareholders and managed by its directors

   (ii)   A company is entitled to own property in its own name

   (iii)   If business is carried on through a company limited by shares, the shareholders can never incur personal liability over and above the amount due on their shares even if the veil of incorporation is lifted

   A   (i) only

   B   (i) and (ii) only

   C   (i) and (iii) only

   D   All of the above

13 In which country are judges appointed at the start of their legal careers?

   A   Italy

   B   Greece

   C   Poland

   D   France

14 Which of the following are **correct**?

   (i)   A contract of guarantee is unenforceable unless it is evidenced in writing.

   (ii)   A contract to sell land must be in writing.

   (iii)   A contract of employment must be in writing.

   A   (i) and (ii) only

   B   (i) and (iii) only

   C   (ii) and (iii) only

   D   All of the above

15 An accountant who double-checks all the calculations in their reports can be said to be protecting their:

   A   Objectivity

   B   Professional competence

   C   Integrity

   D   Confidentiality

16 Which **three** of the following are decisions that would be made by a board of directors?

   ☐   The takeover of a rival company

   ☐   The purchase of a new company headquarters

   ☐   The appointment of a new auditor

   ☐   The appointment of a new management accountant

   ☐   The choice of office cleaner for the company's head office

17 Which of the following is the lowest English Court?

 A   The Court of Appeal
 B   The House of Lords (Supreme Court for the United Kingdom)
 C   The High Court
 D   The Crown Court

---

18 Which of the following statements is/are **correct**?

 (i)   Auditors who provide negligent advice may be held liable for breach of contract by the company which appointed them.

 (ii) Auditors who provide negligent advice to the company which appointed them may be held liable for breach of contract by the company and its shareholders.

 (iii) Auditors who provide advice to a particular person and who know what the advice will be used for may be held liable to that person in the tort of negligence if the advice proves to be incorrect and was carelessly prepared.

 A   (i) only
 B   (i) and (ii)
 C   (i) and (iii)
 D   (ii) and (iii)

---

19 Which of the following examples of European Union law has direct effect on all member states?

 A   Directives
 B   Regulations
 C   Decisions
 D   Recommendations

---

20 Brian has been employed by Wye Ltd for 10 years. His contract of employment states that if either Wye Ltd or Brian wishes to terminate the contract, each party must give the statutory minimum period of notice.

Which of the following is **correct**?

 A   Both Brian and Wye Ltd are entitled to 10 weeks' notice
 B   Brian is entitled to 10 weeks' notice but Wye Ltd is entitled to only 1 week's notice
 C   Brian is entitled to 1 month's notice and Wye Ltd is entitled to 10 weeks' notice
 D   Both Brian and Wye Ltd are entitled to 1 week's notice

---

21 In order to alter the articles of association, the shareholders of a private company need to pass:

 A   An ordinary resolution with usual notice only
 B   An ordinary resolution with special notice only
 C   A special resolution with usual notice or a written resolution
 D   A special resolution with usual notice only

---

22 Where a company has resolved to alter its articles, how many days does it have to file notice of the change with the Registrar?

   A   5 days
   B   10 days
   C   15 days
   D   20 days

23 Which of the following best describes the Companies Act rules on AGMs of private companies with model articles?

   A   Private companies are not required to hold an AGM
   B   Private companies must hold an AGM every year unless the members resolve otherwise by special resolution
   C   Private companies must hold an AGM every year unless the members resolve otherwise by ordinary resolution
   D   Private companies must pass a written resolution each year to dispense with the need to hold an AGM

24 The notice period for calling a general meeting at which a special resolution is to be voted on is:

   A   7 days
   B   14 days
   C   21 days
   D   28 days

25 Which of the following remedies for breach of contract can always be awarded by the court if there has been a breach of contract?

   A   An injunction
   B   Damages
   C   Specific performance
   D   Recission

26 Which professional quality does the accountant display below?

An accountant avoids all situations that they believe could cause a reasonable observer to doubt their objectivity.

   A   Independence
   B   Competence
   C   Accountability
   D   Respect

27 Who is responsible for the corporate governance of an organisation?

   A   The board of directors
   B   The audit committee
   C   The shareholders
   D   The stock exchange

28   Why is it important for an accountant's work to be reliable?

   A   To ensure it is delivered on time and is what was asked for
   B   Because it is a matter of professional competence
   C   To ensure it meets public expectations
   D   To ensure the person who receives the work does not have to check it

29   Under which circumstance does an employer not need to provide an employee with a statement of prescribed particulars?

   A   Where the employee is employed for less than 20 hours per week
   B   Where the employee has received a written contract of employment covering all points
   C   Where the employer has fewer than 20 employees
   D   Where the employer and employee have agreed the statement is unnecessary

30   Which of CIMA's fundamental principles is described below?

   'An accountant should not perform any service that they cannot perform with reasonable care and diligence.'

   A   Integrity
   B   Professional competence
   C   Objectivity
   D   Confidentiality

31   Which of CIMA's fundamental principles is described below?

   'This principle is a combination of impartiality, intellectual honesty and freedom from conflicts of interest.'

   A   Integrity
   B   Professional competence
   C   Objectivity
   D   Confidentiality

32   Which of CIMA's fundamental principles is described below?

   'This principle means not doing anything that might bring discredit to the profession.'

   A   Integrity
   B   Professional behaviour
   C   Objectivity
   D   Confidentiality

33   Which of CIMA's fundamental principles has been breached below?

   A shareholder contacts the company's finance director complaining about the results contained in the management accounts. The finance director replies giving operational reasons for the poor results.

   A   Objectivity
   B   Integrity
   C   Professional competence
   D   Confidentiality

34 Which of CIMA's fundamental principles has been breached below?

A management accountant decides to change the depreciation method used in the accounts without notifying anyone.

   A   Integrity
   B   Confidentiality
   C   Professional behaviour
   D   Professional competence

35 Which of the following statements is **incorrect**?

   A   It is automatically unfair to dismiss an employee for trade union activity
   B   It is automatically unfair to dismiss an employee who becomes pregnant
   C   It is automatically unfair to dismiss an employee who enforces a statutory right
   D   It is automatically unfair to dismiss an employee who refuses to obey a reasonable instruction

36 Consider the English common law concept of *obiter dicta*. Which of the following Sharia law terms is a direct comparison?

   A   Qiyas
   B   Urf
   C   Istishab
   D   None of the above

37 Which of the principles of public life means that accountants should disclose private interests which relate to their public ones?

   A   Selflessness
   B   Openness
   C   Accountability
   D   Honesty

38 Which of the following statements is **correct**?

   A   A breach of warranty allows the innocent party to treat the contract as terminated
   B   A breach of warranty terminates the contract if it is the most equitable outcome
   C   A condition is a term fundamental to the contract
   D   A breach of condition automatically terminates the contract

39 Which of the following statements is **incorrect**?

   A   Contractual terms may be implied by a court to give the contract business efficacy
   B   Contractual terms may be implied by a court to make the contract fair to each party
   C   Contractual terms may be implied by statute
   D   Contractual terms may be implied by trade custom

40 Which of the following is **not** a common law duty of an employer?

    A   To provide work to an apprentice

    B   To behave responsibly towards employees

    C   To provide a reference to employees when they leave

    D   To pay reasonable remuneration to employees

41 The usual remedy for wrongful dismissal is:

    A   Damages under common law principles for breach of contract

    B   Reinstatement

    C   Re-engagement

    D   Statutory compensation

42 Josh contracts to sell a plot of land he owns to Happy Builders Ltd. At the very last minute Josh decides not to go through with the deal. What is the most appropriate remedy for Happy Builders Ltd?

    A   Specific performance

    B   Injunction

    C   Damages

    D   Rescission

43 Which statement concerning the calculation of contractual damages is **incorrect**?

    A   Damages are awarded to compensate the innocent party

    B   Losses are too remote if they are outside the contemplation of the claimant

    C   Claimants must take reasonable steps to mitigate their loss

    D   Damages are calculated by reference to the claimant's reliance or expectation interest

44 Which of the following are sources of international public law?

Select all that apply.

    ☐   Treaties

    ☐   Conventions

    ☐   International customary law

    ☐   General principles of law recognised by civilised nations

    ☐   Any nation's laws which deal with how its citizens should deal with citizens or organisations in other states

45 In which country's legal system would you find delegated legislation called Executive orders and Agency rules?

    A   England

    B   Scotland

    C   Australia

    D   USA

46   James negligently drove his car down a busy high street and hit Sally, who was badly injured. Sally suffers from a rare disease which means that her body takes twice as long to repair itself as a normal person's and because of this she could not work for eight months. As a highly paid city banker she claimed compensation for loss of earnings of £80,000 which is the equivalent of eight month's salary. A normal person would have returned to work after four months. James thinks Sally's claim is excessive, what is the legal position?

A   James is only liable for 'normal damages' in this case loss of earnings for four months calculated on the basis of an average person's earnings.

B   James is only liable for 'foreseeable damages', in this case loss of earnings for four months calculated on the basis of Sally's actual earnings.

C   James is liable for the total of Sally's claim of £80,000 as you must 'take your victim as you find them'.

D   James is not liable for loss of earnings as this is an example of 'financial loss' which is not claimable under the tort of negligence.

---

47   Which of the following is/are **correct**?

(i)   A wrongful dismissal cannot also be an unfair dismissal.
(ii)   An unfair dismissal can also be a wrongful dismissal.
(iii) An unfair dismissal must also be a wrongful dismissal

A   (i) only
B   (ii) only
C   (iii) only
D   All of the above

---

48   Who would normally appoint a managing director?

A   The board of directors
B   The company secretary
C   The company auditor
D   The shareholders

---

49   The appointment of new directors must be approved by:

A   The board of directors
B   The company secretary
C   The company auditor
D   The shareholders

---

50   Fixed and floating charges must be registered with the Registrar of Companies within how many days?

A   7 days
B   14 days
C   21 days
D   28 days

51 Three floating charges have recently been created over the same class of assets. Charge A was created on 10 April and registered on 5 May. Charge B was created on 12 April and registered on 20 April. Charge C was created on 15 April and registered on 19 April. In the event of a winding up which charge has priority?

    A   Charge A
    B   Charge B
    C   Charge C
    D   Charges A, B and C have equal priority

52 If a quoted public company with model articles wishes to issue new preference shares for cash consideration what rule must it follow?

    A   It must offer the new shares to all shareholders of the company in proportion to their existing holding

    B   It must offer the new shares to the other preference shareholders only, in proportion to their existing holding

    C   It must offer the new shares to all existing share and debentureholders

    D   It must offer the new shares to the public via the stock exchange before it offers them to its existing shareholders

53 Which type of company **never** has share capital?

    A   Companies limited by guarantee
    B   Unlimited companies
    C   Private limited companies
    D   Community interest companies

54 In respect of a company purchasing its own shares, what is a market purchase?

    A   The sale of shares by private treaty
    B   The sale of shares using a broker
    C   The sale of shares under the normal arrangements of a recognised exchange
    D   The sale of shares by a placing only

55 Where a transaction at an undervalue is made with a connected person, how much time must pass before it cannot be made void by the company's insolvency?

    A   6 months
    B   12 months
    C   18 months
    D   24 months

56 Which statement regarding public limited companies is **incorrect**?

    A   It must offer some of its shares for sale on a recognised stock exchange
    B   It must have at least one member
    C   It must have at least two directors
    D   It must always have a company secretary

57   Which of the following statements concerning the tort of negligence is **incorrect**?

   A   The standard of care expected is that of a reasonable person.
   B   The same level of care is expected of adults and children.
   C   The claimant must demonstrate 'sufficient proximity' existed between themselves and the defendant.
   D   Where the risk of injury or loss is great, the standard of care increases in proportion.

58   Which of the following is/are **incorrect**?

   (i)   A liquidated damages clause will be void if it amounts to a penalty clause.

   (ii)   A liquidated damages clause will apply where it is a genuine attempt to pre-estimate the loss caused by a breach of contract.

   (iii) A liquidated damages clause cannot be valid if it is for an amount in excess of the actual loss caused by the breach of contract.

   A   (i) and (ii) only
   B   (ii) only
   C   (iii) only
   D   All of the above

59   According to the Combined Code, as a minimum how often should board members stand for re-election?

   A   Every year
   B   Every two years
   C   Every three years
   D   Every five years

60   An accountant develops constructive relationships with their colleagues, and values the rights and opinions that they have.

   Which personal virtue do they display?

   A   Responsibility
   B   Timeliness
   C   Respect
   D   Courtesy

61   Which of the following statements is **incorrect**?

   A   Employees must demonstrate reasonable competence to do their job
   B   Employees must obey all the instructions of their employer
   C   Employees only have a duty of confidentiality regarding trade secrets when they leave employment
   D   Employees have the same duty of fidelity to an employer that they are seconded to as to their main employer

62 What benefits can continued personal development bring to an accountant?

  A Improved communication skills
  B Improved accounting standards knowledge
  C Improved technical skills
  D Improved business awareness

63 Which **three** of the following are matters an accountant should consider when deciding how to resolve an ethical conflict with their employer?

  ☐ Whether they have recently applied for promotion

  ☐ CIMA's ethical guidelines

  ☐ Any internal grievance procedures available to them

  ☐ The opinions of other CIMA members regarding the specific situation

  ☐ The consequences of potential resolutions

64 Corporate governance rules are designed to benefit a company's stakeholders. Which of the following best describes stakeholders?

  A The shareholders
  B Those with an interest in the company's financial performance
  C All those who are affected by the company's activities both directly and indirectly
  D Those who contribute to the success of the company

65 Why is it important for a CIMA member to follow the concept of lifelong learning?

  A To develop their assertiveness skills
  B As the accounting environment is constantly evolving
  C As they are legally required to do so
  D To make sure they are more skilled than accountants from other accountancy bodies

66 Which **three** of the following are **not** included on a statement of written particulars of employment?

  ☐ Right to future pay increments

  ☐ Pension rights

  ☐ Set holiday dates

  ☐ Details of disciplinary methods

  ☐ Job title

67 How does a compliance-based approach to developing an ethical code differ from a ethics-based approach?

  A It sets out fundamental principles for members to follow
  B It attempts to anticipate every possible ethical dilemma
  C It offers general guidelines for specific circumstances
  D Members are expected to comply with the spirit of the code rather than the letter of the law

68   What board structure is recommended by the Combined Code?

    A   The board should mainly consist of executive directors.

    B   The board should mainly consist of non-executive directors.

    C   The board should be structured so no individual or small group is dominant.

    D   The board should consist of executive and non-executive directors in equal numbers.

69   What are ethics?

    A   A set of principles that guide behaviour

    B   Religious rules that determine an individual's actions

    C   The principle that all individuals should work together for a common goal

    D   Professional guidance that guides behaviour

70   Which of the following is **correct**?

    A   A contract is frustrated when something happens after it has been entered into which renders the contract more difficult to perform

    B   A contract is frustrated when a party expressly agrees to manufacture and supply goods and then discovers that they will be far more expensive to produce than he thought at the time of the contract

    C   A contract is frustrated when something happens after it has been entered into which renders the contract impossible to perform

    D   A contract is frustrated if it is impossible to perform at the time that it is made

71   Which body oversees the law concerning sex, religion, belief, age and human rights discrimination in relation to employment law in the UK?

    A   The European Court of Human Rights

    B   The Employment Tribunals Board

    C   ACAS

    D   The Commission for Equality and Human Rights

72   What **three** benefits do non-executive directors bring to a board?

    ☐   They bring in experience and knowledge into the business that the executive directors may not possess.

    ☐   They will support the chairman by pushing through his ideas when other directors challenge them.

    ☐   They can appreciate the wider perspective when the executive directors become involved in complex, operational issues.

    ☐   They ensure the executive directors cannot defraud the company.

    ☐   They provide the executive directors someone to confide in regarding any concerns they have with other board members.

73 CIMA as a chartered institute has what overriding duty?

    A   To provide a source of management accountants to UK and worldwide businesses
    B   To ensure its examinations are demanding for students
    C   To protect the public interest
    D   To improve the quality of management accounts

74 An advert in a newsagent's window read: 'Hoover 2012. £50 ono. Tel: 0208 888 2124'. Karl rang the number and, having enquired about the Hoover said, 'I'll give you £25 for it.' Karl's statement is

    A   A request for information
    B   An invitation to treat
    C   An offer
    D   An acceptance

75 XYZ plc has issued shares on terms that they will be bought back by the company 12 months after the date of issue. What are these shares called?

    A   Ordinary shares
    B   Bonus shares
    C   Preference shares
    D   Redeemable shares

Mock assessment 2
Answers

**DO NOT TURN THIS PAGE UNTIL YOU HAVE
COMPLETED THE MOCK ASSESSMENT 2**

1   D   A register of debentureholders does not legally need to be kept. A register of directors' residential addresses does need to be kept but it is not available for public inspection.

2   A   Frustration only arises where there has been some outside event, for which neither party is responsible, which makes performance impossible.

3   C   The sayings of the Prophet are known as Ahadith.

4   C   Literally 'the reason for the judge's decision.' The actual decision will be specific to the facts of the case and *obiter dicta* are other comments, not legally binding.

5   C   One of the two instances where an ordinary resolution with special notice is required. Whilst a private company can pass decisions by written resolution it cannot remove its directors using one.

6   ☑ An accountant should spend enough time on a job to look into all matters in sufficient detail.

☑ An accountant should refrain from performing services that they cannot perform with reasonable knowledge, competence and diligence

☐ An accountant should only perform work that their employer has deemed them competent at.

☐ An accountant should attend all training and technical update courses available to them even if not relevant to their job.

☑ An accountant should (if relevant) use websites containing technical information to stay up-to-date.

Accountants should not accept work from their employers if they do not believe themselves competent. Accountants are only required to stay technically up-to-date in areas relevant to their current role.

7   C   The profitability of the business is not a concern of business ethics.

8   A   The invoice is a post contractual document, so it cannot introduce new terms without the agreement of B Ltd.

9   B   The most suitable resolution to a conflict may not be acceptable to an employer, especially if the employer is behaving unethically to begin with. No resolution can ensure the conflict never arises again. CIMA is able to give advice to members, not to endorse their actions.

10 ☐ Anne, who worked for 10 years and was given 9 weeks' notice

☑ Barry, who worked for 1 week and was summarily dismissed

☑ Catherine, who worked for 5 years and was given two months' notice

☑ David, who has worked for 18 months and was given a week's notice

☐ Emily, who worked for 6 months and was given 3 days' notice

The statutory minimum notice period of one week for each year of employment is only relevant to people who have worked for one month or more, so Barry does not qualify. Emily should have been given a week's notice and Ann should have been given ten.

11 D   The Combined Code specifically recommends that the roles be separated.

12	B	Shareholders may incur additional personal liability if the corporate veil is set aside, depending on the circumstances.
13	D	In France, judges are appointed as they start their legal careers.
14	A	There is no requirement for an employment contract to be in writing.
15	C	Integrity is the principle of honesty and not being party to the supply of false or misleading information.

16

☑ The takeover of a rival company

☑ The purchase of a new company headquarters

☑ The appointment of a new auditor

☐ The appointment of a new management accountant

☐ The choice of office cleaner for the company's head office

A board of directors will only become involved in major policy and strategic decisions, or where the decisions involve substantial financial commitments. The choice of a new management accountant or office cleaner is unlikely to fall into this area.

17	D	Out of the options, the Crown Court is the lowest in the hierarchy.
18	C	Auditors do not have a responsibility to the shareholders.
19	B	Only Regulations have direct effect on all member states. They come into force in each EU member state without the need to pass national legislation. A decision has direct effect on the member state to which it is addressed.
20	B	Brian is entitled to one week for each year of his employment. The minimum period for an employee to give is one week.
21	C	A private company needs to pass a special resolution with the usual notice or a written resolution with a 75% majority.
22	C	A company has 15 days to file notice of the change.
23	A	Under the Companies Act 2006, private companies with model articles do not need not hold an AGM.
24	B	The notice period for a general meeting at which a special resolution is to be passed is 14 days. The notice period for an AGM is 21 days.
25	B	Damages are always available as a remedy for breach of contract.
26	A	The accountant demonstrates 'independence in appearance'.
27	A	As stewards of a company, responsibility for governance lies with the directors.
28	A	A colleague must be able to rely on an accountant's work meeting professional standards; this does not mean that it does not need to be checked (Option D). Professional competence (Option B) means an accountant has the necessary skills and experience to perform a job, which is different from the work itself being reliable.
29	B	All employees are entitled to a statement of prescribed particulars unless they have a written contract of employment which covers all points.
30	B	Professional competence is described.

31	C	Objectivity is described.
32	B	Professional behaviour
33	D	Confidentiality. Management accounts are for a company's internal use; someone has leaked the results to a member of the public and the finance director should not have disclosed the operational reasons for poor performance.
34	A	Integrity. Changing the method of depreciation without notifying anyone may mislead users into thinking the results are better or worse than they otherwise would have been.
35	D	It could be found to be unfair dismissal (or wrongful dismissal) but refusing to obey a reasonable instruction is not one of the automatically unfair grounds for dismissal.
36	D	*Obiter dicta* are reasons or comments made by a judge in a particular case that may have a persuasive influence on future judges through the concept of precedent. Sharia law has no concept of precedent so there is no direct comparison.
37	D	Where an accountant has conflicting private and public interests they should declare them and attempt to resolve them.
38	C	Breach of a warranty never terminates a contract. Breach of a condition entitles to innocent party to treat the contract as terminated but termination is not automatic.
39	B	Courts will not interfere to correct a 'bad bargain'.
40	C	Employers have no duty to provide references but where they do so the reference must be truthful and accurate.
41	A	The other remedies are available for unfair dismissal.
42	A	As the contract is for land the court may enforce it by way of an order for specific performance.
43	B	Remoteness of damage is concerned with whether the loss arises naturally from the breach and is within the usual course of events.

44

- ☑ Treaties
- ☑ Conventions
- ☑ International customary law
- ☑ General principles of law recognised by civilised nations
- ☐ Any nation's laws which deal with how its citizens should deal with citizens or organisations in other states.

A nation's own laws dealing with other states are international private law.

45	D	The USA has delegated legislation known as Executive orders and Agency rules.
46	C	This is the 'thin skull rule': you must take your victim as you find them.
47	B	A dismissal can be wrongful and unfair at the same time. However, an unfair dismissal doesn't have to be wrongful – the correct notice period may have been given, for example.
48	A	The board would normally appoint a managing director
49	D	The appointment must be approved by the shareholders.
50	C	All company charges must be registered within 21 days.

51	B	Charge B. Although Charge A was created first, it was not registered within 21 days and is therefore not valid. Where correctly registered charges exist on the same class of asset priority is determined by the date of creation, not the date of registration.
52	B	Pre-emption rights apply in the case of shares issued for cash and the new shares need only be offered to shareholders of the same class as those being issued.
53	A	Companies limited by guarantee do not have share capital. Unlimited companies may or may not have share capital.
54	C	A market purchase is made where the shares are to be sold under normal arrangements on a recognised stock exchange. A placing may be used but this is not always the case.
55	D	Two years must pass before such a transaction cannot be void.
56	A	A public company may offer some of its shares for sale to the public but it is only compulsory if it is quoted on the stock exchange.
57	B	Children generally owe a lower standard of care than adults.
58	C	Liquidated damages are calculated differently to normal damages.
59	C	Board members should be re-elected at least every three years.
60	C	Respect. Developing relationships and valuing the views and rights of others demonstrates respect.
61	B	Employees do not have to follow unlawful, unreasonable or dangerous instructions.
62	A	Personal development improves qualities such as communication skills which have to come from the individual.

63

- ☐ Whether they have recently applied for promotion
- ☑ CIMA's ethical guidelines
- ☑ Any internal grievance procedures available to them
- ☐ The opinions of other CIMA members regarding the specific situation
- ☑ The consequences of potential resolutions

The risk of missing out on promotion should not affect an accountant's decision on how to resolve an issue. By discussing their specific situation with others, an accountant will breach their duty of confidentiality and this should be avoided.

64	C	Stakeholders are those who the company's activities affect both directly, such as the employees and indirectly, such as the government.
65	B	Lifelong learning ensures an accountant keeps up to date with technical and other skills that are developed and change over time.

66

- ☑ Right to future pay increments
- ☐ Pension rights
- ☑ Set holiday dates
- ☑ Details of disciplinary methods
- ☐ Job title

The details of pension rights and job title are included on the statement of written particulars.

67	B	The other options describe the framework-based approach to developing a code.
68	C	The board should be balanced to prevent domination by an individual or group. No numbers or proportions are specified.
69	A	Ethics are an individual's principles that guide their behaviour
70	C	In Option B, the doctrine of frustration does not protect someone from having made a (really) bad bargain. Impossibility only becomes an issue at the time performance is required.
71	D	The Commission for Equality and Human Rights oversees the law in these areas.

72

- ☑ They bring in experience and knowledge into the business that the executive directors may not possess.

- ☐ They will support the chairman by pushing through his ideas when other directors challenge them.

- ☑ They can appreciate the wider perspective when the executive directors become involved in complex, operational issues.

- ☐ They ensure the executive directors cannot defraud the company.

- ☑ They provide the executive directors someone to confide in regarding any concerns they have with other board members.

Non-executive directors are there to provide a strong, independent element on the board, not as 'henchmen' to enable the chairman to get his own way. Although the presence of non-executive directors may help deter fraud, they will never eliminate it.

73	C	Chartered institutes have an overriding duty to protect the public interest.
74	C	An advert is an invitation to treat. Karl is making an offer of £25 which, if it is accepted by the advertiser, will comprise agreement.
75	D	They are issued with a view to being repurchased.

Review Form & Free Prize Draw – Paper C5 Fundamentals of Ethics, Corporate Governance and Business Law(12/09)

All original review forms from the entire BPP range, completed with genuine comments, will be entered into one of two draws on 31 July 2010, 31 January 2011 and 31 July 2011. The names on the first four forms picked out on each occasion will be sent a cheque for £50.

Name: _____ **Address:** _____

_____

_____

How have you used this Kit?
(Tick one box only)

☐ Home study (book only)

☐ On a course: college _____

☐ With 'correspondence' package

☐ Other _____

Why did you decide to purchase this Kit?
(Tick one box only)

☐ Have used the complementary Study text

☐ Have used other BPP products in the past

☐ Recommendation by friend/colleague

☐ Recommendation by a lecturer at college

☐ Saw advertising

☐ Other _____

During the past six months do you recall seeing/receiving any of the following?
(Tick as many boxes as are relevant)

☐ Our advertisement in *CIMA Insider*

☐ Our advertisement in *Financial Management*

☐ Our advertisement in *Pass*

☐ Our brochure with a letter through the post

☐ Our website www.bpp.com

Which (if any) aspects of our advertising do you find useful?
(Tick as many boxes as are relevant)

☐ Prices and publication dates of new editions

☐ Information on product content

☐ Facility to order books off-the-page

☐ None of the above

Which BPP products have you used?

Text	☐	Kit	☑	i-Learn	☐
Passcard	☐	Virtual Campus	☐	MCQ cards	☐
Success CD	☐	i-Pass	☐		

Your ratings, comments and suggestions would be appreciated on the following areas.

	Very useful	Useful	Not useful
Effective revision	☐	☐	☐
Exam guidance	☐	☐	☐
Banks of questions	☐	☐	☐
Guidance in answers	☐	☐	☐
Mock assessments	☐	☐	☐
Mock assessment answers	☐	☐	☐

Overall opinion of this Kit	Excellent ☐	Good ☐	Adequate ☐	Poor ☐

Do you intend to continue using BPP products?   Yes ☐   No ☐

The BPP author of this edition can be e-mailed at: stephenosborne@bpp.com

Please return this form to: Janice Ross, CIMA Certificate Publishing Manager, BPP Learning Media Ltd, FREEPOST, London, W12 8BR

Review Form & Free Prize Draw (continued)

TELL US WHAT YOU THINK

Please note any further comments and suggestions/errors below

Free Prize Draw Rules

1 Closing date for 31 July 2010 draw is 30 June 2010. Closing date for 31 January 2011 draw is 31 December 2010. Closing date for 31 July 2011 is 30 June 2011.

2 Restricted to entries with UK and Eire addresses only. BPP employees, their families and business associates are excluded.

3 No purchase necessary. Entry forms are available upon request from BPP Learning Media Ltd. No more than one entry per title, per person. Draw restricted to persons aged 16 and over.

4 Winners will be notified by post and receive their cheques not later than 6 weeks after the relevant draw date.

5 The decision of the promoter in all matters is final and binding. No correspondence will be entered into.